Praise for *Gr*

"I consider Peter to be an elite soccer coach for players of all ages and genders, as he genuinely cares about the player from a holistic point of view. Peter is a true professional with a great sense of humor. He has had a major influence on both the growth and development of the game of soccer in the United States."—**Michael Dickey, director of coaching and player development, Mockingbird Valley Premier Soccer Club; National Coaching Education and Scouting Staff, United States Soccer Federation; and former head coach of Jordanian Women's National Soccer Team**

"As a former youth baseball coach, I was excited to hear that Peter was writing another book. Peter has an incredible depth of wisdom to share with grassroots coaches—insights into how coaches should interact with their players so that learning how to play while experiencing the joy of playing can be achieved by everyone involved. 'A player's mistake is a signal to the coach to where this person can be helped' makes a lot of sense to me. *Grassroots Coaching: Using Sports Psychology and Coaching Principles Effectively* has tons of information and philosophy that would have helped me during my coaching endeavors. This is a book for every coach's library, but there is more here than just advice to coaches. There are thoughts and concepts for anyone who would like to improve their leadership skills."—**Philip Hurley, former youth baseball coach**

"Through Peter's mentorship, I was able to grow my ability to coach and lead a team. He has an incredible ability to break down information into actionable tools and strategies that I continue to use daily. Peter's focus has been and always will be on the players and how we, as coaches, can create an environment where they can become the best versions of themselves."—**Sarah Leiby, Dartmouth College Women's Soccer assistant coach and member of United Soccer Coaches 30 Under 30, class of 2019**

"Peter is a scholar, leader, and educator. He views the educational landscape as an opportunity to set goals for his students and himself, along with a plan to achieve those goals. Making a difference is always a goal for Peter."—**Marcy Weston, Hall of Fame college administrator, instructor, and coach; and NCAA national coordinator of women's basketball officiating (retired)**

"Awesome—a coaching book written by a coach! Peter's wide range of coaching experiences will positively impact coaches at all levels and provide practical insight and strategies. *Grassroots Coaching: Using Sports Psychology and Coaching Principles Effectively* is a resource to help your players and teams grow faster and find real joy in playing their sport."—**John Bonamego, senior coaching assistant, Los Angeles Rams**

"What is the recipe that transforms a good coach into an exceptional coach? For five years, my two boys had the awesome experience of training with Coach Peter, the most exceptional coach we've ever worked with. Energetic and fun, caring and supportive; he is a truly amazing teacher. He helped our boys build their athletic skills while simultaneously building their motivation to put forth their best effort. He celebrated their victories with them and helped them through their tough moments. He taught them the value of being part of a team. Best of all, through the personal connection he was able to create with them, he helped them believe in themselves, which is the greatest gift someone can give to another person. Come to think of it, "exceptional" is not a strong enough word. What word could possibly measure up? All I know is that Coach Peter's positive influence deeply touched our lives, making them better overall, and we will be forever grateful."—**Deb Mead, mother of Sean and Jacob, former TOPSoccer players at Midland Soccer Club**

"In a sports world that has become a bit obsessed with specialization, technical training, and analytics, even for our younger athletes, this book offers a fresh perspective. . . . The authors turn back time and explore how a grassroots approach that helps to build both the athlete's mental and physical skills can greatly improve coaching and teaching effectiveness. I personally have over thirty years of experience in the intercollegiate athletics industry and would recommend this book as a great read for anyone seeking creative ways to rethink their approach to coaching and personal development."—**Kevin Buisman, director of athletics, Minnesota State University**

"Peter J. McGahey and Peter S. Pierro provide a thought-provoking book to help you lead yourself first as a coach, discussing powerful, research-based psychological principles that are proven to lead to success. With this book, you will be able to lead your team and players more effectively. I would recommend this book for any coach who is looking to take their own performance to the next level."—**Cindra Kamphoff, mental performance coach and author of** *Beyond Grit: Ten Powerful Practices to Gain the High-Performance Edge*

"I am excited to dive into this work from Coach McGahey. He is a passionate leader, educator, and voice for coaches of all levels, and his take on the pedagogy of sport is worth your time and energy. During every step of Coach McGahey's coaching career, his focus has been on the holistic development of the athlete. His commitment to education and transformational leadership makes him the perfect person to help coaches everywhere be at their best. Teaching life skills through sport has always been Coach McGahey's superpower. I look forward to continuing to learn from him as he turns his focus from student-athletes to coaches and provides resources for leaders, teachers, and coaches across all levels and sports. As a husband, dad, educator, and coach, Peter has always used his passion to serve others. I have no doubt *Grassroots Coaching* will be a tremendous asset to coaches everywhere as we all search for ways to become the best version of ourselves."—**Joanna Lane, senior director of education and program development, National Fastpitch Coaches Association**

6/16/22
To Ted,
Happy Father's day,
From Barb!
Peter S. Pierro

GRASSROOTS COACHING

Using Sports Psychology and Coaching Principles Effectively

Peter J. McGahey
Peter S. Pierro

Ted
Coaching is a wonderful journey!
Keep Doing Doing Great Things!
Peter

ROWMAN & LITTLEFIELD
Lanham • Boulder • New York • London

Published by Rowman & Littlefield
An imprint of The Rowman & Littlefield Publishing Group, Inc.
4501 Forbes Boulevard, Suite 200, Lanham, Maryland 20706
www.rowman.com

86-90 Paul Street, London EC2A 4NE, United Kingdom

British Library Cataloguing in Publication Information Available

Library of Congress Cataloging-in-Publication Data

Names: McGahey, Peter J., 1973–, author. | Pierro, Peter S., author.
Title: Grassroots coaching : using sports psychology and coaching principles effectively / Peter J. McGahey, Peter S. Pierro.
Description: Lanham, Maryland : Rowman & Littlefield, [2022] | Includes bibliographical references. | Summary: "Grassroots Coaching: Using Sports Psychology and Coaching Principles Effectively explores coaching by focusing on the key tasks of the coach, while providing immediately applicable behaviors and concepts. The responsibilities and privileges of coaching are introduced along with the appropriate accompanying sport psychology and coaching principles"—Provided by publisher.
Identifiers: LCCN 2021053623 (print) | LCCN 2021053624 (ebook) | ISBN 9781475864762 (Cloth : acid-free paper) | ISBN 9781475864779 (Paperback : acid-free paper) | ISBN 9781475864786 (ePub)
Subjects: LCSH: Coaching (Athletics) | Sports—Psychological aspects. | Sports for children—Psychological aspects.
Classification: LCC GV706.4 .M388 2022 (print) | LCC GV706.4 (ebook) | DDC 796.07/7—dc23/eng/20211206
LC record available at https://lccn.loc.gov/2021053623
LC ebook record available at https://lccn.loc.gov/2021053624

♾ ™ The paper used in this publication meets the minimum requirements of American National Standard for Information Sciences Permanence of Paper for Printed Library Materials, ANSI/NISO Z39.48-1992.

A very special appreciation for that gifted musician, loving and caring teacher, friend, companion, and the person who brought us together and connected our shared spirits: Bobbie Bullard Pierro (1934–2017).

CONTENTS

PROLOGUE

Dear Coach,

I am pleased to know that you are learning more about your chosen profession of coaching. Coaching has been an honorable and satisfying factor in my life, and I hope that you find some of my thoughts and feelings to be of assistance in your personal and professional growth.

It was in my third year of teaching and my first year of coaching that I began to connect my sports life with my college school life. I was working on my master's degree and was studying and reading a lot of educational psychology. The course I was taking explored concepts such as attention, closure, awareness, reinforcement, and readiness. I believe that I had what the gestaltists would call a flash of insight—I saw how educational psychology could help me coach my basketball and softball teams.

This was a while ago, and the term "sports psychology" didn't exist. I recall one class session in a physical education course when I was sharing with my fellow students an article from a golf magazine and my use of it in my golf game. The author said that if you were trying to hit a shot over a tree, you should "see" the ball going over the tree and let that image determine your stance and grip, then hit the ball. I told them that I tried it and it worked. I got a lot of funny looks and headshaking from other class members.

Those were the days before Dwight Stones in the high jump, Jack Nicklaus in golf, the Mahre brothers in skiing, and others who were early users of visualization. Now we know about many of the techniques and skills that comprise sports psychology. This book is designed to tell you what some of those techniques are and how they can be used—especially those related to learning theory. You don't need a degree in psychology to use them. In fact, I hope you'll keep saying to yourself, "This is just good common sense." There's sports and there's psychology, and the two fit together very nicely.

And there is so much more to teaching and coaching. You can list many of these things under the title Social Relationships, and you must include "Beliefs about myself" and "People I care about." Above all else, our job as coaches is to deal with people lovingly and caringly as together we learn more about who we are, what we do, and how we do it.

1

OUR VISION FOR YOUTH SPORTS AND YOUTH COACHES

Welcome!

You have taken your first step on the beautiful and wonderful journey of coaching. Few vocations or jobs possess the potential to serve others like coaching. Coaching is about finding ways for others to discover the best version of themselves. Coaching is a gift to others and to yourself: reaching further, going faster, overcoming, succeeding, failing, and finding joy in the journey. Get ready to grow. Get ready to get outside your comfort zone. Get ready to develop people. Get ready! They call you Coach!

Understanding your purpose in coaching is critical. Your *why* matters. Why do you want to be a coach? What is your motivation? Developing a clear sense of your purpose as a coach is imperative. Sports can serve a critical development role in the lives of those who play and compete. As the coach, you set the tone and determine the direction for your team.

Believing in the best in people is imperative as a coach. Too often the assumption is that a coach is present to point out mistakes, highlight weaknesses, and motivate through fear. This could not be farther from the truth for modern-day coaches. Today's coaching is about inspiring, guiding, and growing strengths. Coach people first.

Placing your people first allows you to create a player-centered team environment. A player-centered environment is driven by what is best for each individual player. Our players are our focus. They are our purpose. The players and their long-term growth is our *why*.

The basic purpose of this book is to take the ideas that we have discovered about how people learn and how they operate in this world and to use these ideas to help our kids play the game better and enjoy the game more. These ideas are universal. They are present in everything we learn, and they are present in all sports.

The ideas in this book are not neatly lined up and sequential. In fact, their strength is that they interact and support one another. Repetition might be in focus, and then awareness pops up to help illustrate what we're talking about. Practical activities and examples are used as much as possible to illustrate concepts and scenarios.

We believe you're eager to gain an understanding of the art of coaching. This will be a teaching experience different from any other. Coaching is energizing! Coaching and leading teams is amazing! You're here and you're ready to learn! We are enthusiastic about sharing our passion for coaching with you.

A METAPHOR FROM NATURE

The concept of the team that we use throughout this book is based on a metaphor from the world of nature: the pack and the wolf. This metaphor is that your team is a pack—a pack of diverse individuals with a variety of skills, talents, and gifts. You are part of the pack, and you recognize that everyone contributes. Every member of the pack has his or her own value. Each individual's value needs to be celebrated and grown.

The Wolf and the Pack
Now this is the Law of the Jungle—
as old and as true as the sky;
And the Wolf that shall keep it may prosper,
but the Wolf that shall break it must die.
As the creeper that girdles the tree-trunk
the Law runneth forward and back—
For the strength of the Pack is the Wolf,
and the strength of the Wolf is the Pack.
—Rudyard Kipling, *The Second Jungle Book*

In nature, the wolf pack is dependent on each individual wolf, and each individual wolf is dependent on the pack. The pack consists of different wolves, each one with his own unique talents: one is a great tracker, another is a speedster but tires after a short distance, another is a long-distance runner who plods along but is there when needed, another is the one you want in the final battle, and so on. They all come together as a single, effective force.

Your team is also dependent on each individual player with her unique gifts and talents. Not everyone has the strong arm needed by the pitcher, not everyone has the speed to cover the entire area of center field, not everyone has the hands that can scoop up a sharp grounder deep at short and get it over to first before the runner gets there.

The team functions on the strengths of each individual member. Team members pull together, complement each other, and help develop each member into the best version of themselves. Adversity is tackled together. Victory is pursued together. A pack helps every member of the pack become better.

Sometimes we coaches forget that we are dealing with individual people. Each of our kids is a unique person who must be treated in a unique way. We have to deal with each of them in terms of where he is, how he performs, and what we believe to be the right way for him to improve himself.

Each player needs her team. Only when the team is at its best can the player really express her excellence. Our task as coaches is to make each individual player the best that she can be while helping the team work together as an effective unit.

Note: We will be switching between feminine and masculine pronouns throughout the book. Since this coaching book is about all sports and is to be used by both men and women, we will be using different sports and genders as models at different times—hopefully in equal doses.

THE LEADERS

Everywhere we find people who are in a leadership position. We call them teachers, bosses, leaders, coaches, conductors, directors, and a lot of other names. Regardless of the job, the leader has to bear the basic responsibility for the success or failure of the endeavor.

Have you ever wondered why some leaders are so successful? What does Ms. Temple do that causes her swimming team to make the state finals year after year? What does Band Director Harris do that enables his high school band to be invited to the big Thanksgiving Day parades year after year? What does Coach Sample do that causes players from all over the area to sign up for his summer workshops?

Their teams win games and trophies, but over and above that, they have a knack for creating good players, year after year, players who are highly motivated to work hard, to play hard, and above all, to enjoy themselves as they walk away with the trophies.

What really mystifies us is that those coaches don't know any more about the game than do the coaches of losing teams. Their kids don't run the bases any better. Their kids bat the same way. They throw the ball with the same motions. What's the difference? What did John Wooden do at UCLA that John Doe who coached at State University didn't do? And what did Vince Lombardi say that made the Packers so determined to play their best?

We have heard it said that Coach Wooden was a master psychologist and that Coach Lombardi was a master motivator. That seems to explain why their teams were so successful except that it really explains nothing. What does a master sports psychologist do? And how does a master motivator motivate? And remember that they were successful even when the scoreboard showed that the opposing team had more points at the end of the game.

THE PURSUIT OF EXCELLENCE

If in fact you can be a successful coach even though your team doesn't win every game or every title, then there must be some goal that is higher than winning. Winning will not be downgraded in this book— winning and losing will be examined and evaluated while knowing that given the choice between winning and losing, we'll take winning every time.

There are two goals, however, that exceed the goal of simply winning the game: the pursuit of excellence and the realization of potential. We can point to Peyton Manning, Alex Morgan, Tiger Woods, Venus Williams, and Lionel Messi and show that they didn't win every game, or tournament, or title but they always worked toward excellence in performance, doing the best they could with what they had, and working toward fulfilling their potential as athletes.

Let's examine a few qualities that great athletes exhibit in their pursuit of excellence to gain some insight on how we should lead our teams and players. Here is a short list.

Pride: Your players must be proud of their team, proud of their own actions and achievements, and, yes, proud of you, their coach. In order to be proud, one must have a good self-image, one must have self-esteem. It's hard to hold your head up and say, "I'm an Eagle!" after the coach has spent considerable time convincing you that you'll never be worth anything as a player and as a human being. The pride your players have in their team will be no greater than the pride that each of them has in being a player on that team.

Discipline: Setting goals and then moving toward them with a sense of purpose and responsibility is discipline. Discipline is learned just as the skills of pitching or kicking a ball are learned. Discipline is something that you, the coach, demonstrate as you set rules and keep them, as you schedule practices and get there on time, as you talk about sportsmanship and communicate humanly with everyone. Discipline is the quality that enables a Serena Williams to get to the top of the tennis world and stay there for so many years.

Self-reliance: As coaches, we spend so much time telling kids what to do, what not to do, how to do it, and so forth that we sometimes lose sight of one critical responsibility we have to our players, and that is to make them self-reliant, working with them so that they are self-sufficient, so that they don't need us anymore, so that they become more and more independent.

Courage: This is the ability to assess a situation and then to act in the most positive way possible relative to your goals and your beliefs. We see this daily in people who have lost some ability and simply do not allow that loss to keep them from being the best they can be. We see it in classrooms when a child is determined to learn those numbers and facts and then learns them. We see it in all sports, and when we see it, we see champions.

Dedication and Hard Work: As you spend more time and years in coaching, you will look back and recall that short fellow on your basketball team who seemed to be a magnet for every loose ball or that shortstop who couldn't make a double play pivot until you taught her how to line up the base and the second baseman and then she worked on it and worked on it until it became her trademark.

You also have many roles to play. You must be a teacher and a learner. You can't be one without the other. You will be amazed when you realize how much you have learned and are learning from your coaching and how much you have learned with and from your players.

You also are a leader. You will want to develop the leadership qualities that you will find in many of your players, and the best way to do that is to demonstrate those qualities yourself. This is experiential learning for those you mentor at its best.

And whether or not you want to, you will take on other duties in your coaching role. There are many hats to wear. You will be a counselor, a scheduler, a record keeper, an amateur accountant in some cases, and so forth. Your players will talk to you, tell you things that are important to them. Parents will share important information with you. Confidentiality and common sense will be critical in all of your relationships. And there will be many times when empathy will be asked of you and you must respond appropriately and caringly.

You will be organizing and setting up your team's practice and game schedules. You will diligently keep records and ensure that confidential information is secure. You will be confronted with many decisions that have no direct relationship to how well you teach your shortstop to relay the throw to the plate from the outfield or how well your center boxes out for a rebound. Coaching is a holistic profession: it deals with the whole person (the player), it deals with the whole unit (the team), it deals with everyone involved, even the bus driver—and it deals with you. The business of being a coach brings with it many fulfilling roles.

THE TOP OF THE MOUNTAIN

One of the greatest qualities coaches can have is an ability to inspire their young athletes to do the very best they can. There is more to youth sport than trophies and championships. The most impactful and inspiring coaches often never make it into the newspapers or come up first in a Google search. They are anonymous in the mainstream but famous in the hearts of their players and teams.

You don't have to win a national championship to be an inspiring leader. Dr. Ernie Sturch, vice president of Southeastern Oklahoma State University, was a Bambino League coach for twenty-three years. Over the course of those years, Ernie helped hundreds of kids play their best, but over and above that, those kids always felt their best when he was with them. He cared about every one of those kids and they knew it. He didn't always have the best team and win the most games, but he and his kids were always winners. *That's how it should be and that's how it can be.*

2

LEADING YOURSELF

The Goal—Your *Why*

All right, let's get to the big questions.

- Why do you want to be a coach?
- What's in it for you?
- What are the rewards you expect to get from your service?
- What needs in your life are being filled by coaching?
- Are you gaining something positive?
- Are you avoiding something negative?

Take some time and put your thoughts on paper. Relax and let your subconscious take over. You are at the field, pool, or gymnasium and your team is taking part in an important competition. Back off and observe yourself. Are you enjoying yourself? What are your feelings? Stay with your feelings. Don't let your thoughts get in the way.

THE JOY OF COACHING

Let's look at the different sources of enjoyment available to you as a coach. First, there is the joy of coaching itself. Kahlil Gibran in his book *The Prophet* says, "Work is love made visible. And if you cannot work with love but only with distaste, it is better that you should leave your work and sit at the gate of the temple and take alms of those who work with joy."

Now change a few words: "Coaching is love made visible. And if you cannot coach with love, it is better that you should leave your team and sit in the stands and watch those who coach with love." The holistic development of your athletes should be the focus of your commitment to the coaching profession. Their positive growth as people should be the priority. Being an athlete-centered coach is your mission.

Having the joy of coaching is a choice. You can choose to enjoy it in all of the varied experiences it brings you or you can choose to make it negative in the many ways that are available to you. It is your choice.

THE JOY OF COMPETITION

It is fun to compete with others, to test your strength and abilities against others who can match your strength and abilities—and to see who the best is.

Competing and winning are very interesting concepts, and sometimes we are apt to think that they are the same. Winning a game or winning the championship of your league is a good goal, but without certain necessary elements, the fun of winning isn't there. What must be there is the element of equality or near equality of ability.

In other words, it isn't much fun to win if there's no possibility of losing.

Let's consider a league in which one team is allowed to pick all the star players and goes on to beat every other team in games that are all shortened by a mercy rule. Where is the joy of competing in this case? The fun of the game would be reduced for everyone, including the winners. In major league sports we often hear about breaking up a team that is dominating a league. There are even policies to prevent dynasty-building. In the NFL, the team with the worst record this year will have the first pick in the player draft the following spring.

As adults we often make sure that we have a chance of winning when we play our games. At the first tee on the golf course we compare handicaps and decide which golfer will give strokes to the other. At the bowling lanes we might hear someone say, "I'll spot you twelve pins per game." In a chess match, a superior player might take one of his pieces off the board to make the game more interesting.

If we don't use one of these handicap systems, we adults will make sure that the person we oppose is of comparable ability. Here are two rules of competition as it relates to fun and improvement.

1. If you play consistently with someone who is much better than you, you will improve for a while but eventually you will get discouraged, stop trying, and choose not to compete any longer. You will get tired of losing.

2. If you play consistently with someone who is much worse than you, you will enjoy your victories for a while but eventually you will get bored with it and choose not to compete any longer. You will get tired of winning.

In order to have a good competitive situation, there must be the possibility of losing. If you want to improve, make sure you are occasionally playing people who are better than you and use that as a learning experience. *Without the risk of losing, winning does not have much meaning.*

THE JOY OF LOSING

This leads to the concept of the joy of losing. There are many sayings that describe winning by emphasizing the positive, necessary experience of losing. For example, salespeople say, "Successful people make more mistakes than unsuccessful people." Or a poster on the wall says, "Ships in the harbor are safe but that is not what ships are built for." And how about "Nothing ventured, nothing gained" or "The turtle makes progress only when he sticks his neck out."

We have a friend who was learning to ski. She told the instructor, "I'm doing well. I didn't fall once." Her instructor replied, "Then you didn't try hard enough to improve." Her goal was not to fall; his goal was to have his student extend her limits and improve.

In one important sense, you want to beat your opponent while hoping that he or she is playing well enough to be able to beat you. In order to grow, you must continually challenge yourself. This is not saying that losing is fun. It's saying that the possibility of losing is necessary.

There must also be the possibility of winning. You must enter the arena with the possibility in your mind that you will be the winner. This is not the message "We're number one" or "That other team doesn't even belong in the same arena that we're in." That is your ego talking, and you are setting yourself up to lose with great disappointment and even greater concern for your ability to win in the future. The real message is "We belong in this contest and we will do our best to win this game."

THE JOY OF COOPERATION

Good coaches teach their players to compete with their opponents; great coaches teach their players to cooperate with each other and then to compete with their opponents. It's fine to have your second baseman and shortstop engaged in a friendly contest to see who the team batting leader will be, but it would be great if they shared information about the strengths of the opposing pitcher, and you really want them to be cooperating as they work on double plays.

Teamwork, team spirit, cooperation, playing together, being personally unselfish for the good of the team, these are hallmarks of the excellent teams. Building this attitude and seeing your players come together as a team is indeed one of the joys of coaching.

THE JOY OF SPORTSMANSHIP

Sportsmanship is a concept that's very hard to define. There's a fine line between poor sportsmanship and acceptable behavior. We are in the realm of moral judgments. What is good and what is bad? This is where we are challenged. What we allow our players to do on the field, in the gym, and on the bench demonstrates what our beliefs are about sportsmanship.

The responsible coach must have firm opinions and a narrow definition of sportsmanship as a model of behavior. His players are not allowed to do anything that diminishes their status as high-class people.

They are not allowed to communicate with their opponents in any manner that could be seen as objectionable.

For example, what is the best way to deal with the umpire, referees, or officials on a close call that you think was decided the wrong way; that is, the decision was in favor of your opponent? One of the communication skills we use is to deal with the situation rather than with the person.

Let's set up a situation. The first-base umpire gets caught in a play at second and is out of position to see your first baseman make a tag. From your seat in the dugout you had a better view of the action than he did. He blows the call, and you go out to discuss the matter with him. You could say, "Are you blind? Whoever told you you're an umpire?" or you could question his character by saying, "Well, you're giving those guys this game, aren't you?"

Those comments are aimed at the umpire personally, and his first reaction will be to protect himself. He will deny that his eyesight is questionable and he will be angry because you questioned his integrity and honesty. This exchange has done nothing to deal with the situation.

The other way to go is to say, "My guy made that tag. I think you were out of position. Will you ask the home plate umpire if he had a better look?" In this case you are looking at and dealing with the situation. You may not get the call changed, but you have a better chance. Over and above that, you have shown your players a model of excellence in restraint. (If you go out there kicking and screaming, don't be surprised if quiet little Robin kicks and screams when she is called out on a close play.)

This modeling extends to your relationships with everyone and everything related to the game and the job of coaching. It is in the way you talk to your players, the way you deal with parents, the way you accept a loss, and the way you celebrate a win. You can choose to be a class act or you can choose to be whatever the opposite of a class act is. It is your choice.

MOTIVATING YOURSELF: WHAT'S YOUR *WHY?*

Let's look at self-motivation now and be clear that self-motivation and motivating other people are very different operations. We can't motivate other people unless we are motivated ourselves. Motivation is one of the great builders in our lives. It is concerned mainly with the *whys* of behavior: why do I want to be a coach, why do I want to have a winning team, why do I want my players to be good sportspeople?

Ordinarily our motivation comes from our dreams or our needs. You might say, "I want to be a coach because I have always wanted to be a positive factor in the lives of young people." Or you might say, "I like to be in the spotlight, I have a need to be recognized."

Whatever the case may be, you have stated that you want to be a coach. Motivation is a state within a person that leads to goal-directed behavior. Becoming a coach is a goal, and you are motivated into goal-seeking activity.

This is the essence of motivation. You select a goal that is important to you. You define this goal as clearly as you can. You develop a plan to achieve that goal. When you are very firm and clear that this goal is worthwhile to you, you make a commitment to reaching it. And as you make that commitment, you focus on reaching that goal so there is no room for thoughts of failure. Obstacles are what you see when you take your eyes off your goal.

Reaching the goal is not the important part of the process. The journey, the striving for that goal, is where the joy and the sense of worth are. And just as you are achieving that goal, you set up new and more rewarding goals because the journey toward self-realization and the achieving of excellence are, in fact, the real goals in the life of a growing and successful person. We motivate and we inspire others only when we care enough to do whatever is necessary to reach our own dreams.

BELIEF SYSTEMS

As our coaching journey begins, we have to check three things out. First, what do I believe about myself as a coach? Second, what do I believe about my players? And third, what do I believe about the sport I want to coach? All the decisions made on the practice field and on the playing field are based on your beliefs and values. It's kind of a three-legged stool: all the legs have to be of equal length or you're not on the level.

Beliefs about Coaching

Why do coaches have their players come to a game in neat, clean uniforms? They believe that clean uniforms raise the self-esteem of their players; they believe clean uniforms win respect from parents, umpires, spectators, and opponents; they believe that clean uniforms express respect for the game; and they believe that wearing clean uniforms helps their team play better and win more games.

It is essential that you examine your personal philosophy of coaching. You may already have a coaching philosophy and a set of values based on this philosophy. What is important is that you are totally aware of these beliefs and values so that you can operate honestly, consistently, and assertively.

Here is an example of a teaching and coaching philosophy. These statements become positive affirmations when read aloud.

Belief 1: I love to coach and I love to win and I will coach and win only within the bounds of my beliefs about myself, about my players, and about the game.

Belief 2: As the coach I act as a caring guide and resource person who is committed to assisting each player in growing as a learner, as a player, and as a unique person.

Belief 3: Players learn to play by playing, by being involved in the game.

Belief 4: Any player who comes to practice faithfully, is present at the games, and is interested in being part of the team will be a member of the team, that is, he will not be cut from the team.

Belief 5: The team has to be an important part of the life of each of my players; however, I must keep this in perspective. I must have respect for the other areas of the players' lives: their home and family, school, and any other valued activities such as hobbies, music lessons, and leisure time.

Belief 6: While it is possible that some of my players will go on to higher levels of play in high school, college, or even the major leagues, my task is to deal with them in terms of their present needs and growth. I need to meet my players right where they are now.

Belief 7: My players and I are on the same team. I reject any kind of adversarial, me-against-them relationship. I also expect complete cooperation among all of the players.

Belief 8: Mutual respect is always appropriate and essential. I must present a model for this by respecting each of my players and myself. Also as part of this modeling, I must be an example of other values I subscribe to such as honesty, good sportsmanship, and fairness.

Belief 9: Parents are partners with me in helping children grow and learn in this game.

As a unique person, you have your own beliefs and priorities. What is important is that you take some time to get in touch with them, to evaluate them, and to make sure you are operating within them.

Beliefs about Young Athletes

The second leg of the stool is our beliefs about the young athletes we supervise. Young people love to play games. Maria Montessori, a world-famous educational pioneer, said that play is the serious work of young people. They like to test their physical limits, to see what they can do. They love to be associated with other young people in the enjoyment of the thrill of the game. They enjoy having caring adults share their joy of playing. Very young children will say, "Watch me, Dad, watch me, Mom, look what I can do!" The older ones want Mom and Dad in the stands rooting for them.

Youngsters are seekers; they want to know more about themselves and their chosen game. Each of us has great potential. Our players are in the midst of developing and realizing their potential, and we can assist them in their endeavor. Each of us is a unique human being. We look different, we act differently, and we each bring different skills and abilities to the game.

Young people are dreamers and goal setters. They want to accomplish great things. They have great natural determination that we can squelch or help expand. And finally, youngsters are people with all of the rights and privileges that all people are entitled to.

Beliefs about Your Sport or Activity

This is the third and last leg of the stool, simply and quickly. Any sport or activity is great because it's a fantastic way for people, young and old, to experience the joy of living and playing.

WE GET WHAT WE EXPECT TO GET

Positive expectancy, the positive use of a self-fulfilling prophecy, is the necessary condition for a positive-thinking model. The leader, the coach, must have a firm and fervent belief that the process and the players will succeed, and he must be willing to go the extra mile to ensure their success. We are going to get what we expect to get so let's make sure that we have the right expectations.

Let's add this to the interpersonal communication relationship that we have with our players. Expect players to do well, to practice hard, to deal appropriately with winning and losing and with all other phases of the game. We can treat our players as growing, learning, improving people by using honest, positive comments—or we can do all that inappropriate hollering, cutting down, and demeaning stuff. It's our choice.

Have you ever watched a great coach in action? They expect excellence and they get it. Of course they also operate in an excellent fashion. Here's a brief summary of the qualities players consider the marks of a good coach.

- Good coaches expect us to do our best.
- Good coaches are interested in us as people, not just as players.
- Good coaches have their own goals and share them with us.
- Good coaches are fair; they don't have favorites.
- Good coaches are learners. They know the rules, the skills, how to teach, how to play well.
- Good coaches think well of themselves. That means that they can like us.
- Good coaches communicate well, including listening to us.
- Good coaches are models. They don't just tell us what to do; they show us what to do.
- Good coaches have a sense of humor. They can laugh and have fun and they can even laugh at themselves.
- Good coaches love the game that they are coaching, and they love being a coach.

LEADERSHIP STYLES

As coach of your team, you automatically become the director, producer, and one of the stars of the show. You set the tone, the mood of the game for your team. Coaches can stir up the emotions of the crowd or be the calming influence in some potentially dynamic situations. Coaches have the power and the responsibility to set the stage for a very positive and productive experience for the entire pack.

In this section we are going to deal with leadership styles and the concepts that go along with being a leader—especially self-motivation and positive attitudes—and we invite you to select the type of leadership that is best for you. You may have heard that leaders are born, not made. Not true. Some people are given leadership roles because of who they are, but they keep leadership by what they do. Good leadership is the result of hard work and study.

There are four key concepts that differentiate leadership styles as they relate to coaching.

1. How do I relate to my players?
2. How do I deal with power?
3. How do I interpret the concepts of hard work and improvement?
4. Who has autonomy and decision-making responsibility?

Intertwined in these basic ideas are other important concepts such as motivation, attitude, inspiration, pride, and self-efficacy. These concepts are examined in each of the styles.

One more caution. You may have had a coach you idealized or looked up to but that doesn't mean that you should copy his or her leadership style—it might not be right for you.

Leadership Types and Styles

In the 1930s and 1940s, Kurt Lewin and some of his students did a lot of experimental studies using different models of leadership with children and adults. They identified three basic leadership types: authoritarian, democratic, and laissez-faire. Often the term "leadership type" can be used interchangeably with "leadership style." Three different leadership styles are presented below and then described in terms of how a coach of young players would operate.

The good leader must be familiar with and understand all leadership styles and use the one most appropriate to the persons involved and the circumstances existing at the moment. No one is purely any one of these leadership styles. Although we may basically practice and prefer one model, somewhere along the way we will use all of them.

The Command Style (Authoritarian Type)

The command style of leadership has two related sub-styles, the autocrat and the authority. The command style coach believes that the title "Coach" allows her to make all of the crucial decisions. She has earned or been given the position, and it is up to her to direct the team operation. Being the leader, she is a notch or two above her players. She expects the team to respect her and the position of leadership that she holds. If they won't respect her, they should still respect her office, which she acquired because of her study, ability, experience, or seniority. She will make and enforce the rules. She will also be fair, which she interprets as treating everyone exactly the same.

The Autocrat. The autocrat bases his leadership on power. He sees himself as the boss. He makes the rules because he is the boss. He enforces the rules because he is the boss. In enforcing the rules, he is strict and inclined to use punishment. The way he motivates his players is simple: "Do it because I say so, and if you don't like it, go find another team." There's no nonsense on this team. No fun either. You may have heard the expression "Shape up or ship out." In accord with this, the autocrat will affirm those who follow his commands and warn or punish those who don't.

The autocrat has high standards, and these will be often unreasonable for the young people with whom he is dealing. When they don't live up to his standards, he believes that his players are deficient; for example, they must be lazy, inept, or ignorant. He is sure that they will defy his authority unless he keeps a tight grip and runs a tight ship. In reality, he may be afraid of losing control. He doesn't allow them to get too close to him because if he does, he may get to know them as individuals and that will make it difficult for him to be fair.

Also, he doesn't want people below him in stature and importance to think they are his equal. He isn't big on independent, smart-alecky kids who ask questions and are apt to defy his authority. After all, it's "My way or the highway!"

Ordinarily the autocratic coach will not communicate with parents. There's a problem here because it complicates the question of who's in charge. If he does hold a parent meeting, it will be strictly to inform them of his rules, what he expects from them and their children, and to let them know in an unsubtle way that he is the coach, the only coach.

There is an important element to note about the autocrat coach: the autocrat coach has to be a winner. Otherwise he will lose power and will feel that no one is backing him up anymore. People tend to only support the autocrat coach as long as he is winning. When he loses the power struggle, he wants to fade into the woodwork. The defeated autocrat coach tends to become the avoider coach (see disengaged style below).

The Authority. The other command style is the authority. The authority bases her leadership on her expertise. She is the coach because she is the best person for the position. She has learned and is learning the skills, the rules, and all other aspects of the game and of coaching. She also has made a study of people and how they operate, including child and adult psychology.

The authority sets the rules for the team. She knows what the players need to do. She establishes the structure and culture. She enforces the rules and motivates her players through the use of punishment and compliment.

As the leader she is responsible for player and team standards, expectations, and goals. From her position of authority, she can set up a transactional relationship with her players. She can play Let's Make a Deal with them: "Do this . . . and you will receive this . . ." or "Don't do this . . . and you will receive this . . ." It's a simple transaction. Behavior is rewarded or punished based on successful completion of the task and according to the authority's standard.

The transactional approach can be effective in the short term, but results achieved in the short term often can prove costly to teams and individual players in the long run. The cost of pursuing short-term results can be non-authentic coach-player relationships; the loss of an individual player's hopes and dreams; and the revelation that each player is only a pawn in the coach's pursuit of her personal goals.

An authority is higher than her followers who are at various stages of ability and achievement and need her assistance in order to improve. She is not "one of the girls" but she is an expert in communication and listens to and considers whatever anyone tells her. She also has no trouble explaining her rules and decisions to the players if they ask. She is fair in that she considers the situation logically, looks at all of the consequences, and then makes an expert decision in terms of the needs of the player or the team. Respect is expected simply because that is how teams operate effectively.

The authority will communicate with parents. She will sit in the stands for a chat and will have meetings with them. She is not worried about who the boss is. She usually is pretty secure about herself and what she is doing. She is a constant learner and always studying. The authority knows that she is the authority. This is not ego—it's just plain fact. Telling the truth is not bragging. Others will be impressed with her knowledge of the game and of young people.

Transformational Style (Democratic Type)

The transformer coach believes that his players are equal in status to him. He gets his power from the players he represents. Everyone has some positive thoughts or actions to bring to the organization and it would be a loss if some people were not heard. The coach and his players respect each other, and this respect is for people rather than for positions or titles.

This coach feels that it is important for him to communicate with each of his players one on one. He gets to know each of them as well as possible so that he can deal with them on an individual basis. Mutual respect is not only desired but also cherished. His players understand that he will make decisions differently for each of his players.

A holistic approach to development is the norm for the transformer coach. He strives to positively inspire and motivate his players by teaching them new skills and strategies while moving them outside their comfort zone. Transformer coaches lead with enthusiasm and optimism.

A transformer coach believes in each individual player. Challenging standards are established and intrinsic motivation is cultivated. Players are encouraged to try new skills and strategies. Failure is accepted and understood as part of the learning process. Players and coach face failure and adversity together, as a pack. Support and feedback are given as players are encouraged to take risks and challenged to be innovative problem solvers.

A positive and collective vision for the team is communicated by the transformer coach. He strives to motivate others to do more than they originally intended and often more than they thought possible. The transformer coach is driven to help his players be motivated to combine their efforts for the benefit of the team.

The transformer coach sees the group as the basis for decision making and wishes to have his players become active in the process. Team rules are made, shaped, and enforced by everyone in the operation. In order to be fair, he considers the person involved and the circumstances and then makes his decision on an individual basis. For this reason, fairness means treating everyone differently according to the needs of the person and the team.

The transformer coach is prepared to equip his players with the skills, strategies, behaviors, and values that build champions on and off the field. The path to mastery and becoming is to walk alongside his players, developing the person, encouraging the struggle, offering guidance and support. His goal is to co-create environments that will mold his players into great people as well as great athletes.

Disengaged Style (Laissez-Faire Type)

Last, there's the laissez-faire type of leadership. This is a disengaged style of leadership with two associated sub-styles, the avoider and the delegator. "Laissez-faire" is a French word meaning "to leave alone." This leadership type is different from the others and it can operate at the perceived ends of the leadership spectrum. The responsibilities of coaching don't magically change or diminish for the disengaged coach. She is still responsible for her players and teams and yet she may choose to delegate or not to act.

The Avoider. The avoider coach has the responsibilities of coaching but ignores the responsibilities of leadership. He will show up at practices and games only to roll the ball out. Lots of scrimmages are played without instruction or guidance. He lets the players take over, and he takes a position wherein he isn't responsible for what happens.

The avoider coach may be completely inactive, and he likely will avoid getting involved when critical decisions need to be made. This means key decisions are not made and actions are often postponed. Communication tends to be shallow and overly optimistic.

His players may be having fun. After all, they are playing their game. But the avoider coach wants to put everything on cruise control. Instruction that helps his players acquire new skills and strategies takes a back seat. Guidance tends to corrective actions if anything at all. Ownership of his players' and team's growth and maturation is missing. Players may feel stress because they don't really know what to do.

The avoider never establishes an authentic relationship with his players or team. Respect is not an issue since there is no relationship to base it on. There really are no rules or enforcement, while standards are often low and unclear. Everyone just goes along to get along. And fairness has very little meaning since no one is in charge who can act in a fair or unfair manner.

The Delegator. Oftentimes the delegator coach will be low profile or even misunderstood. The delegator coach has a clear understanding of her individual responsibility to the organization. She is confident of her leadership and coaching abilities. This clarity and confidence allow her to assign responsibility and accountability to others. In other words, she delegates.

After responsibility and accountability are given, the delegator coach trusts her people. She is not looking over their shoulder all the time. Room to be creative, to explore, and to develop solutions is provided. Availability and encouragement are hallmark behaviors. The delegator coach is available for questions and to provide guidance. She offers verbal and nonverbal reassurance and praise.

The delegator coach can almost be invisible at times. Her ego is secure. She believes she has surrounded herself with quality and talented people. The talents and skills of others need to be grown and supported. The team and organization develop based on the best efforts and intentions of everyone.

Communication with players, coaches, and the team is consistent. Authentic relationships are built. The delegator coach supports players in making key decisions and while helping to shape team culture. She says, "I have so much faith in you and your ability that I'm going to leave you alone, give you space, and I will be here to support you when you need me." This style can look weak and illogical, but in combination with other styles it is very powerful.

The delegator assigns assistant coaches real areas of responsibilities and permits them to do their job. Parents are encouraged to participate in the pack appropriately with feelings of autonomy and fulfillment.

When everything is going well the delegator coach may appear disengaged. However, when things aren't going well, the delegator coach is very visible. She is confident of her skill set, with a strong conviction and vision for her team. She will not use the power of her leadership position until she is needed. Then she will stand up, confront, and communicate. She'll set out standards, accountability, and processes very clearly. She will become the authority.

Leadership Affirmation

Coaches lead. That is what they do. They lead in a dynamic environment, and their responsibilities go beyond the Xs and Os. Their leadership is focused on people. Guided by their beliefs and values, they will select the appropriate leadership style for the situation and circumstances. *The required leadership style will change as the need changes.*

3

LEADING THE PLAYER

Good coaching is tough. It's complex. It demands study and thought and a commitment on your part. You may have been a fine player and know all the skills. That doesn't guarantee success. Many star athletes have bombed as coaches. And many coaches who have never starred as players have risen to spectacular heights as a coach. What are the common ingredients and what are the factors and knowledge you need to be an expert coach? Let's look at some essentials.

CHRONOLOGICAL VERSUS DEVELOPMENTAL AGE

Chronological age and developmental age are two important concepts to understand. All players have a chronological age. He is five years old. She is fifteen years old. Chronological age is based on the birth year of the player.

Developmental age is more complex. It is an estimate, and it takes into account the physical, mental, and social maturation of the individual player. Here are two examples. A young player is ten years old in chronological age, and she has just experienced a growth spurt. The growth spurt makes her taller and more coordinated than her peers, which means she is older developmentally. Or a high school player might be sixteen years old chronologically, but he has not yet experienced puberty. Because he might be shorter and less physically developed than his peers, he is therefore younger developmentally. Individuals develop at different rates and in their own time. Developmental age can impact a player's performance on the field and their experience with the game. Note: Girls typically develop earlier than boys at every stage.

Coaching and playing conditions must be set in relationship to the physical, mental, and emotional development of your young players. Developmental age matters. Physically there may be great differences in their development even if they are the same age. A child may have a lot of energy, but when he runs out of steam, he comes to a complete stop. His fine muscle control will not be fully developed, and he will be a bit awkward. It would be a mistake to expect adult physical performances from him.

Individual players grow socially from a self-centered attitude to a group attitude. Teach them cooperation and don't get bent out of shape when your second baseman chases the runner all the way back to first and doesn't throw the ball to the first baseman or when a young player reaches down and picks up the soccer ball with his hands. Remember that they learn by doing and they haven't done a lot yet. They also learn by watching but they haven't seen many rundowns or soccer games in their lives.

Don't overlook the late, or slow, bloomer. She is developing and growing at her own rate. She is learning at her own readiness level. And don't be overly infatuated with the earlier developer. It is easy to rely on the earlier developer to win games and overlook his skill development and strategic understanding. After all he is bigger and faster than his peers. Teach him the game too. All players regardless of their current developmental age deserve investment and insight from the coach.

What Do These Kids Want Anyway?

Youngsters in their fantastically honest way are pretty clear about what sports are and how they would like to be involved. In a survey done in Australia by the Youth Sports Institute, boys and girls were given twenty possible reasons for participating in non-school sports, and the twelve most chosen were ranked as follows.

1. To have fun
2. To do something I'm good at

3. To improve my skills
4. To play as part of a team
5. To stay in shape
6. To experience the challenge of competition
7. To get exercise
8. To learn new skills
9. To make new friends
10. To learn new games
11. To get involved in team spirit
12. To win games

Yes. For both boys and girls, "To win games" came in twelfth place. They felt very strongly that all members of the team should have an equal opportunity to play. It was more important for all members of the team to play than for the team to win. Learning to play the game was more important than winning. Now you try. How would you rank the same twelve choices?

_____ To have fun
_____ To do something I'm good at
_____ To improve my skills
_____ To play as part of a team
_____ To stay in shape
_____ To experience the challenge of competition
_____ To get exercise
_____ To learn new skills
_____ To make new friends
_____ To learn new games
_____ To get involved in team spirit
_____ To win games

In addition to these, the children answered the question, "What advice would you give to adults involved in children's sports?" They replied in this order:

1. Don't yell so much.
2. Teach us more.
3. Let us be more involved.
4. Let us express ourselves more.
5. Don't have favorites.

6. Encourage us more.

Defining Fun

Fun is important to the young people playing our games. Young people naturally love to play games. They like to test their physical limits to see what they can do. They love to learn new skills. They love to be associated with other young people sharing in the enjoyment of the game.

Let's dive deeper into understanding the ingredients of fun from the player's perspective. Visek, Achrati, Mannix, et al. (2015) examined the topic of fun. In this study, researchers asked young soccer players and their parents to define fun.[1]

Using concept mapping, the study identified 4 fundamental tenets of fun in youth sport within 11 fun dimensions composed of 81 specific fun determinants while also establishing a youth sport ethos. The four fundamental characteristics of fun found by the researchers were contextual, internal, social, and external.

According to the researchers, the three most important dimensions of fun relative to the others were

- positive team dynamics (social)
- trying hard (internal)
- positive coaching (external)

These three connect and correlate to form a trifecta of related dimensions to promote and support fun in practices and games (contextual).

Visek, Achrati, Mannix, et al. (2020) approached the topic from a different angle. This time fun determinants were explored within the global context of sex, age, and level of play.[2] These contexts are typically how youth sports are categorized.

The results of this study confirmed that the findings of the original study held true regardless of sex, age, or level of play. This study's findings supported early evidence that girls and boys regardless of age or level of play agreed on the relative importance and defined elements of the determinants of fun.

Fun Elevates into Joy

Playing the game should be fun for the kids, and just as importantly, coaching should be fun for you. On this we can agree. However, sports offer another level of emotional experience for the participants. That next level is joy.

Joy is found in sports. People venture into the world of sport to share and experience games in all their splendid beauty. The attraction of beautiful games is joy. Players play and coaches coach to discover and experience joy. The fun we're having transcends into the joy we all experience.

Joy comes alive through powerful life experiences. Joy lies within the journey of playing sports—and within the journey of life, for that matter. The thrills of the challenges, the new discoveries, the successes, and the failures of playing sports allow joy to blossom. We carry these joyful experiences from sports with us for the rest of our lives.

Maturation and the Way We Play:
A Colleague's Creative Experience

> We have to be aware that there are different levels of maturation that it takes to play our simple to complex games. I had an interesting lesson in maturation and competition in my first year of teaching kiddie PE. I was teaching in a K–6 school so I had to be creative about my gym setups.

> One time I had the volleyball net up for the upper grades and, of course, kindergarteners and lower-grade kids couldn't play the regular game of volleyball. So I invented a game for them that I called Clean Up Your Own Backyard. I got out fourteen playground balls and divided the kids into two teams. I put seven balls at the back wall on each side of the gym. I said to the kids, "When I blow the whistle, start throwing all the balls on your side over the net to the other side. Clean up your own backyard. When I blow my whistle again, stop, and we'll count how many balls are in each backyard." Not a bad idea.

> They went to work. They were throwing, chasing down and fielding the balls, and getting good physical activity. Everyone was on his or her own, scrambling, throwing, chasing, yelling. When I blew the whistle, they stopped and then . . . they all simply jumped up and

down and hollered. They didn't count how many balls were on each side of the net as I figured they would. The game was over and wasn't it fun! Which side won? No one noticed. Let's do it again!

One day the sixth graders came into the gym early and the game was still on. "Hey, Coach, can we play that game?" several of them asked me and the rest said, "Yeah, how about it?"

So I said okay, and they went at it. Was it the same game? Not on your life. It was a completely different game. They had to choose up sides. The leaders said things like "You play back and try to catch the balls" and "Get rid of the balls quick."

When I blew the whistle after five minutes, the action stopped and the counting began. The winners cheered and the losers said, "Let's play again."

There are three simple points here. (1) Young children are not concerned about whether they win or not—the joy is in the playing of the game. (2) Older children are more invested in winning and at this age they understand that in order to win you have to have cooperation among the players. The pack is important to the wolves. (3) The joy of playing the game remains at all times and at all levels.

—Herb Price, K–8 PE teacher

ARE WE SPEAKING THE SAME LANGUAGE?

Gyms and fields are alive with communication. Players are cooperating and competing. Our games represent a dynamic switchboard of interactions.

As coaches we play an important role in this communication process. We need to be keenly aware of the language we are using and the messages we are sending. Decisions made by the players are based on our instructions and communications.

When working with young players and even high school players, we are often working with players experiencing skills, strategies, and competitive environments for the very first time. It may be the first time a player is performing what we're teaching. Players also bring their own unique learning styles to our team.

Telling, showing, doing—all these are important coaching communication strategies to use in reaching our players. All our actions contain a message for our players. Choose wisely.

Clarity is a must. Unfamiliar coaching jargon or terminology needs to be avoided. Players just won't understand it. Game-based communication is key. Instruction needs to be connected to the actual game the players are experiencing. Draw on reference points from your observation of practices and games.

Encouraging independent decision making in your players is critical to their long-term understanding and enjoyment of the game. Joystick coaching needs to be avoided. Overcoaching and the constant shouting of instructions does not permit player decision making. Players are often paralyzed by joystick coaching and overcoaching. Translating and applying our coaching messages in the heat of the action is nearly impossible.

Players must be encouraged to play and then receive instruction and feedback in the appropriate manner and at the right time. A player immediately and intimately involved in the action is not ready to receive guidance or instruction.

Let's look at some real-life examples and see what the coach expected and what the players did. A coaching friend tells this story about a Tee-ball game he was watching.

One of the little fellows, let's call him Joey, was on second base when the next batter got a hit. He ran to third and stopped dead (you know how that is). The coach jumped up and down and yelled, "Go home, go home!" The little tyke just looked at him and the coach kept jumping up and down and yelling, "Go home, go home!" Well, that did it. Joey started crying and ran off the field, into the stands, and into his mother's arms.

Pretty dumb, huh? Of course not. It made sense to Joey and that's the only thing that really matters. The coach assumed that Joey knew some things about the game that Joey didn't know. After all, he's five years old and this is a new experience in his life. Even if Joey had seen a hundred games, he might not have had the background foundation knowledge to understand what the coach was saying. Sometimes we think kids learn things by standing around and inhaling the information. The problem is, they don't. The best way to learn is by playing the game.

Thirteen-Year-Old Has-Beens

Let's take a look at the messages we give our players about their future in the world of sports. How soon do we give them these messages? How strong are these messages? What are our goals as we give our kids these messages?

It has been well documented that 70 percent of the children who start in organized sports at a very young age, five or six years old, will drop out by the age of thirteen. Sports is no longer fun. Ralph Wolff, speaking on the chronology of an athlete's physical development in *Coaching Kids for Dummies*, states his case in this interesting way.

- Hey, you ought to see my three-year-old swing a baseball bat! He's a natural! But then again, I've been working with him since he was six months old.
- My little girl just fell in love with figure skating and wants to compete in the sport. But she's already eight years old. Is she too old to start training now?
- Our seven-year-old doesn't seem to have much interest in sports. Should we just give up on him in terms of athletics?

These are the concerns of some parents who believe that their kids are washed up or has-beens if they aren't playing sports and starring in them by the time they're eight or nine. They seem to believe that if a youngster doesn't get on the fast track in sports at an early age, their chance to develop into a high school, college, or professional athlete will simply vanish.

Sandy Fischer, former softball coach at Oklahoma State University, was asked about this, and she said,

> I didn't care to scout a player or contact a coach until the player I was interested in was in the junior year in high school. Kids mature at different ages and there are kids who top out at twelve years of age and others who reach maturity at a later time. By the junior year, most players have attained a pretty good level of maturity and I got a pretty accurate idea of what their future on my team would look like.

Many coaches are concerned by the narrow experiences of the one-sport athlete. There is so much carryover from one sport to another that is valuable in terms of skills, attitudes, teamwork, and game strategies.

For another reason, spending all year on one sport (league games, tournaments, travel teams, clinics, etc.) can get really exhausting (even boring).

Why not try soccer or track, tae kwon do or tennis, golf or volleyball in the off season? Try out the world of sports and see what fits.

There are many benefits in being a multisport athlete. The diversity of movements helps develop underlying athletic skills. Exposure to different teammates, coaches, game models, and learning environments helps to strengthen a player's capability and adaptability. Burnout and overuse injuries can be limited by rotating a player's learning and sports environment.

Experiencing many different sports environments allows for an exciting discovery process. This discovery process encourages maturation and learning. Without exploration the player may never know where her greatest abilities and interests are. Specialization comes later, once passion, maturity, and skill have intersected appropriately.

Positive and Negative Goals

Children, just like you and me and everyone else, have goals that determine their behavior. The concepts stated here agree with work that was done by Rudolf Driekurs and Albert Adler. They asserted that the child's behavior is based on his search for significance within a social setting—in this case, his place on a team.

Positive goals are beliefs and actions that are acted on by the child to achieve a desired place on your team—a place that they hope to have. The child's behavior is in agreement with the behavior that has been determined to be necessary to attain the goals of the specific social group. In other words, he is acting in a manner that enables him to belong to and contribute to the group.

Negative goals are beliefs and actions that are turned to and acted upon by children who feel that they are not being allowed to reach their desired place on the team—a place that they deserve to have. The person's behavior is in conflict with the behavior that has been determined to be necessary to attain the goals of the specific social group. That is, she is acting in a manner that doesn't allow her to belong to or contribute to the group. Table 3.1 lists common behavior goals.

Negative goals are simply positive goals that have been turned inside out. They're not really different, they're just a difference in the perception of the player. And this perception results in a different reaction and action as the player attempts to reach goals.

It is important that we realize that misbehavior in one group could be acceptable or even desirable in another group. We are dealing here specifically with an athletic team. Therefore it is imperative as a coach that you establish clear and consistent behavior expectations and boundaries.

Below are generalized descriptions of the behavior associated with each of these goals. These are indications of behaviors that may be impeding growth. Note the difference between wants and needs. And be careful not to put labels on individuals as you process and recognize their behavior.

Positive Goals

Acknowledgment: I want to be acknowledged for what I do and for who I am—give me a pat on the back, a smile, a "Nice job," a nod, any action to let me know that you know that I exist and that you care about me, about who I am and not just about what I do on the field.

Acceptance and Belonging: I want to be accepted, to be a member of your team. I want to belong to something worthwhile. I want to be sure that I am a member of this team. I qualify for membership simply by being on this team.

Justice and Fairness: I want to be treated as an individual person and to know that I will be on an equal basis with everyone else on the

Table 3.1. Positive and Negative Goals

Positive Goals (+)	Negative Goals (-)
Acknowledgment	Attention
Acceptance and Belonging	Power
Justice and Fairness	Ego Fulfillment
Involvement	Inadequacy
Autonomy	Revenge
Community	Preference
Accomplishment	Assumed Disability

team. I want to trust you that you will be fair to me and to everyone else. I will respond by being fair to you, by trusting you.

Involvement: I want to be a contributing member of this team, and I want to help make this team the best it can be in every way I can.

Autonomy: I want to be heard when I have something important to say. I want to help this team by giving positive, helpful suggestions.

Community: I want to belong to a positive, caring peer group, to be a member of a great community. I am willing to be a responsible, contributing member.

Accomplishment: I want to be a success. Success for me is doing my very best to achieve the goals I've set for myself as an individual player and as a team member.

Negative Goals

Attention: I need to be noticed a lot so I will make sure you pay attention to me and to what I am doing. I will behave in such a way that you will not be able to ignore me. I have noticed that if I misbehave in any way, I will get your attention, so I will figure out some ways to really bug you and you will have to give me your attention.

Power: I need to be able to take over sometimes, to tell people what to do, and to be able to do whatever I want to do regardless of what is best for me or for the team. If I have to fight for it, I will.

Ego Fulfillment: I need to have people tell me how good I am. If they don't, I will remind them of how great I am. If you don't tell me how good I am, I will believe that I'm not an okay person or an okay player.

Inadequacy: Sometimes I need to leave the playing field when you want me to do something that I'm not good at. I don't like to be made fun of by my teammates and by my coach for my poor playing.

Revenge: I don't like what you are doing to me. I'm going to make you uncomfortable for treating me this way.

Precedence: I'm supposed to be given precedence in games and at practices because I'm better than the rest of those girls. After all, I'm the girl who wins the games. That makes me special, so I should get special privileges.

Assumed Disability: I really don't like that I never get to play, and I'm not getting anything out of this game. I'm going to quit without really quitting—I'm going to forget my soccer shoes or I'm going to act as if I'm hurt or I'll pretend that I don't care about not getting to play.

Fun Elevates into Joy

The command coach will never figure out what's going on with the kids and will get into trouble because she will not notice the differences in how they express positive and negative goals. Actually, she probably won't care about the way the kids are operating and what they want. She will probably consider negative goal activity to be misbehavior that should be suppressed with punishment.

The transformational coach will take advantage of the knowledge he has about each of his unique players and use it to help them succeed in having a significant position on the team and in the game. He will be inclined to interpret negative goal activity as cries for help and to use appropriate means to help the child. How do I take advantage of understanding the unique goals of each player? I keep learning and growing.

Note that with positive goals, the term "want" is used. With negative goals, the term "need" is used. Most often when dealing with positive and negative factors, we are concerned with entirely different factors.

In this case, however, we are dealing with differences in quality and in quantity. The player with a negative goal needs more of your time and your empathy than the one trying for positive attention. She needs a higher and deeper level of interpersonal interaction.

All the goals listed above will be acted out in some form of behavior. In your interactions with your players, you will be promoting the achievement of positive goals. Along with your players you want them to be acknowledged for who they are and what they do. You want them to feel that they belong in your organization. You want them to feel that you are being fair in your dealings with them. You want them to be involved in the process. You want them to have power in the process. And you want them to have some measure of success in the endeavor.

The problem facing the coach then is in identifying which trait is being acted out and then dealing effectively with it. One way is to learn all you can about how people operate in this world (and don't ever be surprised when they act strangely). One very valid way is trusting your gut. Does this sound right? Does this feel right? Note the gut feelings in the following scenarios.

Attention and Acknowledgement: A Scenario

Ben Johnston has been a member of the Adams High School Basketball team for two years. He is far from being one of the stars. In fact he gets into the game only when the Rockets are either far ahead or far behind. Since he is a junior there is a possibility that he will do better next year. But that is next year. One function he has this year is playing defense against the starting point guard during practices, and he really gives the guard fits. He is very valuable in that role but the game crowd doesn't get to see that.

Head Coach Schmid has his eye on Ben but Assistant Coach Clark spends more time with him. They are aware of Ben's abilities, and more than that, of his dedication to the team. So they acknowledge his presence constantly during practice and during the game. They make it a point to speak to Ben and other subs when it is appropriate. This is not a gut feeling. It's more of a heart and head process.

Attention and Power: A Scenario

Betty Irving is the biggest star on the Adams High School volleyball team. She is a senior and working on her fourth varsity letter. In fact, she has seniority over Head Coach Laura Brovelli, who is in her second year at that position.

Betty feels that she, Betty, ought to have more to say about all aspects of the game than Coach Brovelli allows her. A few of the other seniors on the team lean in that direction. Coach Brovelli observes this, and trusting her gut feeling, she knows that it is a potential problem. What to do?

Coach Brovelli has been around a while and has seen coaches confront their players using the my-way-or-the-highway approach and knows that some not-so-good things can happen with this approach, including parents getting involved in the wrong way.

What does Betty want? She wants to run the team. She wants power.

Recognizing this, Coach Brovelli sets up power relationships for Betty. During practice Coach Brovelli says, "Betty, will you help Assistant Coach Myers work with Karen, our new setter? Her old team didn't use their setter the way ours does." During a game she says, "Betty, make sure we give Kay more chances. The defense is weaker on her side."

Then after a game she says, "Betty, I like how you reacted to that change in their offense."

So during the practice sessions and during the games, Coach Brovelli gives Betty more and more power opportunities. To underline this, give your player that power as often as you can but never do it when he or she is demanding it. In other words, reward appropriate behavior and ignore inappropriate behavior. Catch your player doing something right.

Attention and Demanding: A Scenario

Mel Owens has been ignored for a long time. He's not good enough to be on the court and he's too good to be cut. And he doesn't like being ignored though he may not have a conscious awareness of this feeling. His inner being notices that when he does something that the coaches don't like, they holler at him—that is, they give him their attention. So whenever the need for recognition gets strong, he does something aggravating. He notices that the coaches yell "Stop that!" when he keeps bouncing a ball. Here is the order for attention and response.

1. Doing something right and being rewarded.
2. Doing something wrong and being punished.
3. Being ignored and accepting it.

So in terms of our needs, we would rather be punished for doing something wrong than allowing ourselves to be ignored—to be a nonentity. Much of what we call misbehavior is actually a plea for attention.

Community and Belonging: A Scenario

Kay Howard, a junior, has just transferred to Adams High School and has joined the school's volleyball team. She came from a small-town high school and is a good prospect for the team. She is concerned about how she will be welcomed here. The team has a good record in the conference and they have several returning players, including juniors, who played on the sophomore team last year.

It is the first meeting of the team. Coach Brovelli is speaking, and among other things she says,

On this team we have some players returning from last year, some players moving up from the sophomore squad, and even a few transfers. As you know, we have a wolf-and-pack belief system. You are all unique individual players and you are all members of the pack. Each and every one of you is a member of the pack. In your portfolio you have a copy of "The Wolf and the Pack" and a copy of your rights and responsibilities.

All positions are open—each of you has the opportunity to earn any position that you choose to try out for. I believe that every one of your coaching staff has shown that she is fair in her decisions.

There are no strangers in this room and there are no bullies in this room. We win a lot because we work with one another, we communicate with one another, we trust one another, and we care about one another.

"Knowing how to get information is more important than storing facts."—Henry Ford

LEARNING IS THE PROCESS

Learning is the basic process. Teaching enables learning to take place. We focus on teaching facts and concepts so much that we fail to see what the process really is. When you teach a fact or concept, you want someone to agree to learn it while having the ability to learn it. You can't teach anyone anything unless that person agrees to learn and is capable of learning. Learning is wanting to receive a fact or concept and having the ability to receive it. Nothing may happen when you teach a fact or skill or idea to your players, but something always happens when your players learn a fact, skill, or idea.

Learning is an active process, and the learner must be actively involved. It is goal oriented and purposeful. The learner's interest in the task is a good indicator of his readiness to learn. Pay attention to the player who asks questions. He is displaying his interest and you know that he is motivated to learn and to grow. Learning is its own reward. That player doesn't need a smiley face, but he will be pleased to get one.

When you are coaching (teaching), it is essential that the learners (your players) be really interested in what you're presenting. "Will this help us win the game this Saturday?" "Will this help me kick the ball farther?" "Will this help me clear that bar?" Learning occurs best when what is learned can be applied by the learner to his own life.

Fortunately for us coaches, learning is improved and accelerated when the player is in communication with people who are significant to her, such as a coach, just as teachers and parents are significant to her in other circumstances.

Here's a master principle: Learning how to learn is the most important goal of education. You learn how to learn only by being involved in the learning process.

Becoming a better teacher and coach is realizing that your players have the power of deciding what they are going to learn. Reward them for what they have learned or punish them if they don't. And the choice still exists, choose to learn or not. Gain the reward or suffer the punishment. A real choice.

Push harder for meaningful learning—not the stuff you memorize. The real stuff that is important to you and me as people. That's when learning and teaching come to life.

Let's pick up on one of the facets of the Australian study discussed above. The kids in the study said that good coaches teach them how to play. Here are some principles of good teaching and coaching.

Ownership: It's Your Choice

If you want your players to be responsible for their actions, then you must let them make decisions. They shouldn't be responsible for your decisions; that's your job.

Stan the Star decides that he is so important that he doesn't have to run laps like the other guys. You tell him that he will run those laps but he still doesn't think you should make him do that. When you tell Stan the Star to make up his mind to run laps just as the rest of the players do or suffer the consequences, you're telling him that this is his problem not yours and he's going to have to make a decision. The ball is in his court. This is called ownership of the problem.

Now the critical issue has to do with Stan's perception of the problem. He would like to blame the coach, thinking, "Coach won't let me take batting practice," but he is being forced to make a decision and he will have to deal with the consequences. He might think this: "I refuse to run laps so I guess I won't get to bat." Or he might think this: "I want to bat and in order to do that I have to run laps so I'll do it." It's his problem, his decision.

Along with ownership are the natural consequences that we all deal with. For example, if you choose to try to drive on an icy street, you may end up hitting a tree. In coaching, we deal with logical consequences. We make rules such as "You don't throw your bat because someone could get hurt." When Jane threw her bat, she broke a rule and she must suffer the consequences. Now then, what do we do? Have her run laps? Have her do pushups? Make her rake the infield? None of these corrective actions are relevant because they are not related to the offense. The punishment must fit the crime. Jane misused the bat and she will not use a bat again until she gets a lesson on the correct use of the bat (which of course she already knew and chose not to demonstrate).

Readiness

The older your kids are, the more they are able to do and to learn. Is that too obvious? Many coaches try to teach skills and strategies that their children are not ready or able to learn. Your job is to learn what children at your players' developmental age can do generally and then to learn about the individual readiness of each of your kids. For example, your neighbor's son Frank and your son Curt are the same age. Frank is able to field a ground ball and Curt isn't ready to do that yet. Curt is okay and should be treated that way. Let's wait for him to catch up.

Major work in education was done by behaviorists led by E. L. Thorndike. The task for teachers was expressing Thorndike's concepts in ways that could be used in the classroom with kids. When we are working with a child in learning a task or a process such as subtraction, shooting a jump shot, or serving a volleyball, we usually define three kinds of readiness that the child may exhibit in doing that task.

Here is how that psychological statement may look on the court or field or arena.

1. If Curt is ready to learn how to use his feet to control a ball and he is allowed to do that, he will have a happy experience.

2. If Curt is ready to learn how to use his feet to control a ball and he is not allowed to do that, he will be frustrated.

3. If Curt isn't ready to learn how to use his feet to control a ball and he is forced to do that, he will have a negative, perhaps even a traumatic, experience.

Number 1 is an ideal situation. Curt is ready to go—you are ready to have him go—and everyone is happy. We are usually dealing with this kind of situation. The Curt in this case will continue to play the game— he will not become a dropout.

Number 2 happens quite often. Curt is ready to learn to play soccer and he wants to use his feet on that ball but someone or something is standing in his way and he is feeling unhappy about the whole business. Have you ever sat on the bench, itching to get into the game, and the coach ignored you? Maybe he said you weren't ready but you knew you were ready? Note that the word "frustration" is the correct psychological term for this condition.

The Curt in this case has choices that he and his support system may make. Shall I stay and hope the situation will improve? Can I be moved to another team? And there's a bigger question: Should I give up on this situation and game and do something different—drop out or, perhaps better said, be pushed out?

Number 3 is the really scary one and yet coaches and parents have seen it many times. This is the one that brings out the verbal abuse and the insults. Curt is just not able to use his feet that well and his coach and parents are not okay with that. They do not want him to do something that is better for him. They keep pushing him, abusing him, saying things like, "You're not even trying" and "Larry down the street can do it and he's two months younger than you."

They are not willing to wait a little while until Curt has developed physically to the point where he can do the task. Curt has experienced those traumatic episodes in which Mom and Dad pushed and shoved him to do things and were abusive to him, making him feel guilty or an embarrassment to his family when he wasn't able to do them.

Curt doesn't really have much choice in his continuing in the game. He is not mature enough to simply say, "I don't want to do this anymore. I want you to let me drop out. I want to do something else." One common tactic is to assume a disability: "My foot hurts when I kick the ball" or "These shoes hurt my feet." This an example of psychological withdrawal.

In the psychology of learning, this represents a two-by-two matrix, and there has to be a fourth type of readiness. So here is the fourth type of readiness applied to sport: If Curt isn't ready to learn how to use his feet to control a ball and he is not forced to do that, that is okay and Curt is okay.

Reasonable, intelligent, and caring coaches and parents accept Curt right where he is and deal with him in terms of what he can and can't do. Curt is safe and still in the game. He doesn't need to assume a disability and he won't become a dropout. Curt will play the game and learn and find joy (see table 3.2).

Kids come to sports at all stages of physical, mental, and emotional readiness. There are things they are ready to do and learn and there are things they can't do and learn at that specific time. Recall the story about Joey and his going home from second base. That little person was ready for some things but his baseball vocabulary and his conceptual knowledge of the game weren't up to dealing with that situation.

A lot of overcoaching goes on. A coach stands in the third-base coaching box giving elaborate signs, trying to teach youngsters intricate pick-off plays, and demanding fancy pitches. The simple fact is that children are not at a stage of development that allows them to learn all the things we have learned over twenty or more years of playing. Each player is at his or her stage of development. They are where they are and not where we would like them to be.

The expert coach knows his skills, he knows his players, and he matches them up. The child playing tee-ball was ready to do some things on the field but he had a little problem with knowing about going home. His coach needs to be an understanding and caring person.

Table 3.2.   The Readiness Matrix

I. Curt is ready.	III. Curt is not ready.
We help him do it.	We try to make him do it.
He has a good experience.	He has a negative experience.
II. Curt is ready.	IV. Curt is not ready.
We keep him from doing it.	We don't make him do it.
He is frustrated.	He's okay and that's okay.

"Everybody is ready; it's up to you to find out what they are ready for."—James Hymes

So we expect kids to know strategy, rules, and skills that we have spent years learning. And then when they don't know these things, we get on them about it. This is a big issue with parents and some coaches. "Why doesn't he run the cutoff play when the other team has runners on first and third?" "What is she doing? She should serve into the back corner." "Why isn't he making the outlet passing there on the fast break?" It could be as simple as the player not having learned that yet. We have to teach kids what they are ready and able to learn—and not before but also not after. Teach your players what they are ready to learn and when they are ready to learn it. Not before. Not after. This is the art of the master coach.

Dealing with Mistakes

The message we often give our players is that not only is it not okay for them to make a mistake but if they make a mistake, they are not okay.

Ten-year-old Joan has just begun taking tennis lessons with a new coach. She has learned from her less-than-positive home, sports, and school experiences that you are not supposed to make mistakes and if you make a mistake, that's something to be ashamed of. Even her former tennis coach, who worked with Joan when she began taking lessons at age eight, was one of those people. Let's join Joan and Cathi Jensen, her new coach, as Cathi helps Joan with her serving.

"Okay, Joan, hit a few serves."

Joan does her best to show her new coach what she can do and then she asks, "How did I do? Did I do it right?"

"It looked pretty good to me. Now let's try this. Toss the ball up a little more to your right side—I think that will let you get a better swing . . . Yes, that's better, how did that feel?"

"It felt good."

"Great. Now I'd like you to swing a little harder."

"If I do that I might not hit it in the right place."

"That's all right. Let's just see how it works."

This goes on with simple adjustments, constant positive reinforcement of good attempts, and no put-downs for bad attempts.

Now comes the end of the lesson.

"Coach, did I make many mistakes?"

"No, we were just trying to get better all the time. Were you trying to make mistakes?"

"No."

"Were you doing your best?"

"Yes, but . . ."

"I saw you doing your best. You can be proud of yourself for what you did. I will see you at our next session."

Children do not perceive the difference between making a mistake and being a mistake. But making mistakes is an integral, essential part of learning. If you are not making mistakes you are not pushing the limits and therefore you are not growing. It's the same on the baseball field, the soccer pitch, the basketball court, the volleyball court, and the football field. A mistake is a signal from the learner to the coach that says, "This is a place where I need help."

Involvement

Learning how to play is an active, involving process. You learn best by doing, by playing. The younger the players are, the truer this is. There is a lot of difference between telling an eleven-year-old or an eighteen-year-old to sit on the bench and watch how Henry swims, serves, or swings.

Remember this lesson: "Anything worth doing is worth doing poorly at first." The idea is simple and inspired. When Joan plays tennis for the first time, she will, by adult standards, play poorly, and that's not only okay, that's the way it has to be. Tennis is worth playing and it will be played poorly by Joan . . . at first.

Recognizing Uniqueness

One of the things we are sure of is that each of us is a unique individual and different from every other person who has ever lived. We all want to be treated as something special, and certainly each of us is special. We have to keep reminding ourselves, however, that in dealing with others, in this case our players, each of them also is special and wants to be accepted as someone who is special.

Fact 1: Every person is unique in many ways.

Fact 2: Every person in many ways is the same as every other person.

These facts confront us as coaches. We try to teach the same thing to everyone and it works—to some extent. We also teach everyone differently according to each one's natural movements, and this also works. Everybody is different. We don't all bat the same, shoot the same, run the same, or throw the same. Identify and appreciate these natural differences and take advantage of them. Yes, there are basics, but we don't need carbon copies. Appreciate the differences and take advantage of them. You will win more games with players who are becoming the best they can be instead of players who are busy making sure they're doing everything the right way (your way).

Just imagine what might have happened if a coach had told Michael Phelps he shouldn't let his arms move away from his body on his down stroke or Patrick Mahomes II not to move his feet when he threw or Megan Rapinoe to change her flowing movement into more practical, choppy steps when she shot the soccer ball.

The best we can do is help each of our players become the best person and player that he or she can possibly become.

Motivation

Ben's grandfather set up a horseshoe pitching area in the backyard. He and young Ben had a lot of fun playing with it. Now Ben is out there this morning pitching the horseshoes all by himself, and his dad will play with him this evening.

This is intrinsic motivation. The energy and desire to play comes from the game itself and from Ben's interest in it. Ben isn't competing against anybody out there. He isn't trying to please his dad and mom. He isn't doing it because his grandfather told him to. He isn't expecting anything from anyone, not a pat on the back, a piece of candy, a raise in his allowance, or any other external reward.

He is enjoying and experiencing the game on his terms. He is a kid enjoying a game that a kid his age and size can enjoy. He is experiencing the joy of playing.

Contrast that kind of motivation and interest with what can often be seen in youth sports—what is called extrinsic motivation. This is motivation that comes from outside the activity and the individual. Some coaches use the term "negative extrinsic motivation." The command coach says, "Do what I want you to do or you're going to be sorry." Fear of punishment or consequence is the lever for action.

Some coaches are a bit more enlightened and use positive extrinsic motivation: "If you stay on the team and practice, I'll give you a nice uniform, a pat on the head, recognition on social media, or whatever it takes." Elements outside the individual player or the game entice them to act or behave in a desired way.

There is a transactional nature to external motivation, a do-this-and-get-this deal made between coaches and players. It can work in the short term and it's marginally better than the negative stuff, but be careful because it can boomerang on you. Some kids catch on to how the deal works and say, "What do I get if I do that?" and "I scored a goal, so give me something." Working only for or toward a reward has removed the internal motivation for the player. The reward itself is the carrot for action as opposed to strong internal feelings.

Cultivating intrinsic motivation in each individual player is important. Co-creating environments in our pack for each player to be the best version of themselves permits intrinsic motivation to grow and thrive. Fueled by their own passions, players commit to practicing and playing at another level. When the pack is working together and when conditions exist for intrinsic motivation to blossom, good things happen.

Goal Setting: SMART Goals

Individual players need to have their own goals and dreams. This is natural and normal for all teams. We as coaches need to support and encourage each individual player's aspirations. Players should set positive personal goals.

A player's goals will create a pathway to follow. The coach then guides and assists each player along their path. Goals should be set or established; for example, "This is who I am" and "This is what I need" and "This is where I want to go." Establishing positive personal goals fuels intrinsic motivation.

SMART goals are a common process tool for setting and establishing goals. They are:

- **S**pecific and clear, detailed, and applicable to current circumstances
- **M**easurable and quantifiable in order to track results and chart progress
- **A**ttainable and challenging and possible
- **R**ealistic and relevant given current constraints and circumstances
- **T**ime-bound

Rights and Responsibilities

One of the most important processes in the whole coaching operation is the use of rights and responsibilities. In the appendix is an example of rights and responsibilities for you to reference and print for your team. Our packs are made up of individual players. As a member of our pack, each individual player has certain rights. And just as important, each individual player has responsibilities to the other members of the pack. These are opposite sides of the same coin. This is a critical relationship dynamic to understand.

A player's rights and responsibilities become a true operational procedure for how your pack collectively functions and thrives. A player's actions, attitudes, and choices are guided and shaped by their rights and responsibilities. Within this framework, coaches shape their players' behaviors. Rights allow coaches to see clearly what each individual player needs whereas responsibilities illustrate the behavior and attitude an individual player must show to be a welcome and highly effective member of the pack. Rights and responsibilities establish agreed-upon standards.

Our standards serve as a process roadmap. The rights and responsibilities allows you to focus on necessary behaviors and attitudes. Being in agreement with each player permits you to stay on the issue and not on the player. An environment of growth and excellence is co-created.

If you and your players are doing everything right, the result is experiencing the joy of playing your sport. If there is no joy for the players and no joy for the coach, then the coach is in the wrong place and doing the wrong thing and it's time to change. *That's how it has to be.*

NOTES

1. A. J. Visek, S. M. Achrati, H. M. Mannix, K. McDonnell, B. S. Harris, and L. DiPietro, "The Fun Integration Theory: Toward Sustaining Children," *Journal of Physical Activity and Health* 12 (2015): 424–33.

2. A. J. Visek, H. M. Mannix, A. Chandran, K. McDonnell, S. C. Cleary, and L. DiPietro, "Toward Understanding Youth Athletes' Fun Priorities: An Investigation of Sex, Age, and Levels of Play," *Women in Sport and Physical Activity Journal* 28 (2020): 34–9.

4

LEADING THE TEAM

No player can outperform the team. A team truly in sync is a thing of beauty. The interaction between teammates is seamless. They are flowing and creating the game together, committed to and enjoying bringing out the best in each other. The pack shines.

Remember, the law of the jungle states that the strength of the wolf is the pack, and the strength of the pack is the wolf. The strengths of each individual player combine to create the strengths of the team. Synergy between teammates is critical for a high-performing team. Teammates play and compete with and for each other. Games and practices are tackled with a real sense of everyone's individual and collective strengths.

High-functioning teams are collaborative. There is no direct competition between teammates. That is saved for the opponents. Teammates are not your opponents. They are members of your pack. Collaboration comes in the form of understanding and commitment from each individual player while understanding that individual strengths are required to bring out the best in their teammates and team. This consistent application of strengths is accompanied by a deep commitment to being the best player *for* the team as opposed to being the best player *on* the team.

The best version of you brings out the best version of us. Collaboration means helping others become and discover the best version of themselves. It means tackling adversity and challenges together. It means recognizing that mistakes, whether individual or collective, are signals for improvement. It means co-creating a clear plan for ever-improving performance. It means everyone is committed to making the team better.

We want to create high-performing teams. We are driven to have our teams do well. Developing and understanding the pack mentality allows us to form a positive and collaborative team culture. This provides the opportunity for everyone to intentionally live our established team standards. Living our standards creates an important team spirit and sense of community.

The pack mentality appears to run counter to our current, contemporary, individual-first-and-always culture. In other words, what can I get for myself versus how can I serve my team, my neighborhood, my community, or society as a whole? This is one of the main challenges we face as coaches today.

Before we offer insights and strategies for leading your team more effectively, let's take a brief look back at the evolution of youth sport from the days of community and neighborhood programs to the current professionalized models.

THE WAY IT USED TO BE

When we were youngsters, we did almost all of our game playing in our neighborhood. There was an empty lot across the street from our house and we played baseball, basketball, and football there. Kids came around to our place and sometimes we went to their lots.

In the evenings, adults took their kids to see other adults play baseball and football in the parks and basketball in the school gyms. Kids never played any of their games at night under the lights or in the gyms. Adults were participants in the games, not spectators. The kids were the spectators, dreaming about the time they would be old enough to play on a real field or court. They had a lot of adult heroes to watch live on the field (there was no television).

Some towns and cities had good recreation programs for the kids. We had two parks with ball diamonds. The park director started baseball programs for kids at the parks. He set up two age-group leagues. The park furnished the bats and balls and the catching equipment. We didn't have uniforms. We played only in the mornings and in the afternoons. Two high school kids made their summer money by organizing the leagues, taking care of the field, and umpiring the games. There were no adult spectators.

Moving up to playing sports in the high school was a big thing. You got uniforms for the first time. You got to play on a real field, a real diamond, a real basketball court. You got real coaching from a real coach and not just your big brother or your friend's big brother. You got to play teams from other schools. And perhaps above all else, your parents came to see you play.

Girls' sports? Not very much and certainly nothing interscholastic. What a waste of good athletic talent! In some cases, there was a very negative reaction by adults toward "tomboys." Girls simply were not supposed to be involved in sports.

After World War II, returning veterans got into sports very heavily and especially softball, which had been played in camps and bases all over the world. The sports field was still dominated by adults. Adults played the games under the lights and the children were the spectators. They watched adults play and they learned about sportsmanship, they learned how to deal with opponents and officials, they learned the rules and strategies of the game, and they learned what winning and losing meant. Hopefully, we acted as adults and they observed and experienced us from the child's viewpoint. They had models to emulate.

This is directly opposite from what is happening today. We've moved away from children learning through watching adults' behavior.

The Big Change

In 1939, Carl Stotz of Williamsport, Pennsylvania, started a baseball league for kids ages eight to twelve and modeled it after the major leagues. He made rule changes such as shortening the distance between the bases. It was for the kids, so it was named Little League. It had a slow start because the United States entered World War II in 1941.

After WWII, we did not limit children's sports and activities to baseball. Football, basketball, soccer, and all other sports were recognized and developed. And the kids started off earlier—some as early as age four. Girls' sports started slowly, but when the parents of talented girl athletes demanded that these girls be allowed to play in Little League, we found that we could develop significant sports programs for girls. Title IX was coming.

As children grew up, good playground facilities and strong local recreational programs for them were established, mainly with the parents of the players acting as coaches. The next step was having kids get into Little League and other regional and national sports programs. This created coaches who stayed on long after their kids moved on—a kind of non-parent, career coach. We now have organizations and non-parent coaches in almost every sport that our young people are involved in.

The sports scene for kids today is completely different. When was the last time you saw a bunch of kids get together on their own to play a baseball game? Or a soccer game? Or any game?

Title IX

The Title IX clause of the 1972 Federal Education Amendments was signed into law on June 23, 1972. It states that "no person in the United States shall, on the basis of sex, be excluded from participation in, be denied the benefits of, or be subjected to discrimination under any education program or activity receiving Federal financial assistance." It has received the most attention for its impact on athletics, especially at the collegiate level. In 1975 the U.S. Department of Health, Education, and Welfare issued a final interpretation of Title IX, which mandated that educational institutions provide equal opportunity to men and women in athletic programs. In 1980, the U.S. Department of Education was given the responsibility of overseeing compliance with Title IX through its Office for Civil Rights.

THE SPORTS SCENE NOW

The organization of kids' sports games is very complex now. Essentially we have added new elements to the game. We have coaches and assistant coaches for all of our teams. Some of them are trained to work with children; some of them are not. Some are interested in the kids; some are interested in themselves. Some are knowledgeable about the game; others are not. Some have patience and understanding; others have short fuses. Some like dealing with parents; others hate to deal with them.

As for the parents and guardians of our players, some know the sport, its rules, its strategies, its nuances, and others don't. Some have patience with their children; others don't. Some see that the purpose of the child's involvement is the accomplishing of the child's goals; others see that the purpose of the child's involvement is the accomplishment of their, the parents', goals and aspirations.

And it is all organized. The kids don't play for the fun of it. They play to win, to get medals and trophies, and to go to the regional and state tournaments. And they play in prime time so that the spectators can be there for whatever reason they have for being there.

The children are playing the games and the adults are the spectators. Adults and coaches are telling the kids how to behave, how to deal with opponents and officials, how to play the game, what the rules and strategies are, and what winning and losing is supposed to mean to them. The kids are expected to deal with all these aspects of their game in a very serious, adult manner. At their age they have not observed their mother, father, older siblings, aunts, uncles, or anyone else playing the game so they cannot use these experiences as models for their own behavior.

These changes to the playing models have brought about a shift in the learning environment. This shift has placed more responsibility on coaches. Coaching roles have expanded. Coaches now teach the fundamentals skills and strategies that kids used to acquire playing in their neighborhood or observing their elders playing. Teams provide recreational opportunities for kids who aren't moving as much and teach kids how to compete and play appropriately without relevant models. Coaches strive to create joyful playing experiences in a highly structured and often overly competitive environment.

And yet with all this added responsibility, our goals as coaches remain fundamentally unchanged. Sports teams matter in the lives of the players. Coaches are there to help them become the best people and players possible. They are driven to create positive and high-functioning teams. Coaches are responsible to their pack.

Your pack is more than a collection of individuals—it is a system of relationships among its players and coaches. You, your assistants, and your players form a unit that you call the Eagles or the Lobos or the

Aces. This unit must have a set of goals that is agreed upon and acted upon by the individual members. Without this set of goals, you have a group of individuals. With this set of goals, you have a team. In team sports, cooperation always precedes competition.

Cooperation Is the Partner of Competition

It's a competitive world out there. Teach these kids to fight their way to the top. Otherwise, they are going to be stepped on, walked over, overlooked. They will become losers. That's how adults often present the world of competition to the kids. Our teams need to be clear on how they are going to deal with competition as all of us work together.

This is one of those issues that we approach differently with our kids than we do with ourselves and with other adults. Adults deal in competitive ways in very few situations, and when they do, they make significant adjustments in how they will compete.

There are times in adults' lives when there is no doubt about being fully cooperative and when no competition is involved. The players must cooperate completely in order for the organization to be successful.

The essence of cooperation is having people work together toward predetermined goals. This is the essence of the team. It's essential that the individuals involved communicate openly and clearly with one another. They must work cooperatively. They can't fall into the trap of hiding their discoveries or ideas so that they can one-up their associates. If they do, the whole project is in jeopardy. (Can you imagine the string section of the orchestra competing with the woodwinds or one bassoonist battling another?)

John Wooden, the fantastic coach of the UCLA teams that won so many NCAA titles, never talked to his players about beating their opponents. He demanded that they work together as a team and that each of them become a better player today then he was yesterday.

> A player who makes a team great is more valuable than a great player. Losing yourself in the group, for the good of the group— that's teamwork.—John Wooden

Teamwork

Our packs are built on the strengths of each individual player working cooperatively with one another. Our packs are playing for and with each other—not against. There are a lot of good slogans hanging on locker-room walls such as "There is no *I* in *team*." Yet we have all had to deal with those self-centered persons who are quick to remind us of their great accomplishments. Direct talk usually isn't very effective with them so let's come at it from another direction.

Coach Hudson has been dealing with Billy the Boaster throughout the season. Billy, who says, "But there is an *m* and an *e* in *team*," makes a big interception that helps his team get back into the game and eventually win. He isn't letting anybody forget what he did and how he dragged the team from the jaws of defeat. Let's listen in as Coach Hudson deals with this issue during the after-game session.

Coach Hudson: Well, we pulled that one out of the fire. You guys played a great game; you hung in there until we were able to make some breaks. Let's take a look at a real turning point—that interception in the third quarter. Who made that interception?

Everyone looks at Billy, who has no trouble smiling, waiting for the accolades. However . . .

Coach to Team Captain Ned: What did you do on that play?

Ned: I got around my blocker and put some pressure on the quarterback.

Coach: Don, how about you?

Don: I shut down the tight end—he never got into his pattern.

Coach: Carl?

Carl: I broke through the middle and kept the quarterback from stepping up into the pocket.

Coach: Zach?

Zach: Brett and I had the end on our side covered.

Coach: Really well done. And we had the center of the field covered by some of you other backs. Okay, Bobby?

Bobby: The quarterback got away from Ned. I poked his throwing arm.

Coach: Billy?

Billy: The pass was short and wobbly and I stepped in front of the end and caught the ball.

Coach: And you made a good run with it. Okay. Let's answer my question. Who intercepted that pass?

Ned: It sure looks like a lot of guys did a lot of good work.

Coach: That's right. That is what we call teamwork. We all do our job right and good things happen. The real mark of champions is that they all do their job as well as they can and nobody worries about who gets the credit.

> It is amazing what you can accomplish if you don't care who gets the credit.—Harry S. Truman

COMPETITION IN THE ADULT WORLD

It really is a funny thing about competition. Adults talk about having to compete in the real world, and they are very clear about when and how they, themselves, are going to compete in their real sports worlds. There are some very distinct rules and models that must be followed. Unfortunately, adults reserve most of these rules and set-ups for themselves while they expect kids to live and play by the rules and beliefs expressed in the big league model. Here it is, plus a few other models that adults have created for own experiences in the world of sports.

The Big League Model

This is *the* model, the model most people have in mind when they talk about competition. This is the model that is often believed to be needed to produce professional athletes. Children play from pre-K through high school, college, the minors, and finally the best make it into the majors.

Throughout this process, those who don't measure up are dropped or drop out. If you're not good enough, you're cut from the squad. The players are separated into those who belong and those who don't belong. Don't let the poor players get in the way of the progress of the good players. If they can't cut it, they're history. Adults like this model, especially if they are winners in this game.

The Flight Model

Each year many golf and tennis clubs have championship matches. Some of them set up "flights." The best sixteen players are in the championship flight, the next sixteen are in the first flight, the next sixteen in the second flight, and so on until all members of the club are included and everyone is competing at a level at which he can win. This means everyone has the possibility of being a winner. We adults like this one.

The Handicapping Model

The team Sarah bowls on is in a league that uses handicaps. If Sarah's team averages 800 and your team averages 830, you have to give her team a spot, or handicap. Usually this is two-thirds of the difference between average scores, so your team gives her team a twenty-pin spot per game. This makes the competition fairer than a head-to-head contest, and each team has a better chance to win. We adults like this one too.

The Special Olympics Model

The Special Olympic philosophy respects each person regardless of his or her disability. When you watch the Special Olympics, you see each child doing his best in whatever event he has chosen. Each contestant is acknowledged for his efforts. Everyone is a winner because winning is the reward for risking and participating. We adults like this, and we should.

The Road Race Model

There are many road races open to the public in large cities and small: the Boston Marathon, the New York Marathon, a 10K race in Oglesby, Illinois. Anyone who wants to can enter, so there are the stars going for number 1 and your third cousin Sandy going for the fun of it. There are disabled and aged people competing. No one is eliminated; the lights are left on for the late finishers as long as they finish before the race course closes. Participants are successful or unsuccessful according to their own goals, their expectations, or their PR, their personal record. We adults like this, and we should.

The Festival

Some team sport organizations set up festivals for their players. The festival environment is an attempt to simulate neighborhood and community playing experiences. Players are all involved in age-appropriate games. Playing time is maximized to improve engagement time, skill development, decision making, and fun. Results and standings are not kept. Individual players are regularly rotated between teams. They play with and alongside many other players throughout a festival. The focus is on the joy of playing, learning through the game, and being a great teammate. We adults can be skeptical of this one. We should love it.

THE CULTURE OF THE PACK

Open any contemporary book on sports or business and you'll read about culture. Listen to any interview of a championship team and you'll hear about culture. Go to work, go to church, volunteer in your community, be a member of your family, and you'll experience culture. Culture is *all* around us. Everyone seems to know more about culture then we do. What is this mysterious thing called culture? How is it developed? What are some of the key ingredients?

Ask any coach at any level to describe how they want their pack to function and be together. Each coach will tend to use the same words: "hardworking," "committed," "fun," "teamwork," "sportsmanship," "positive," "supportive," "high standards," "challenging."

Not many coaches would use words like "negative," "cut-throat," "ambivalent," "lazy," "mean-spirited," "selfish," or "no standards" to describe their ideal pack. As coaches, we all want our pack to operate in a similar and positive fashion. This is our culture. It's the way we do things around here. Just as the people on a team are not static, neither is culture. Culture is alive. It is always changing and growing, progressing or regressing.

Envisioning the culture that you want for your team is only the first step. The more challenging step is developing and living that ideal culture. This takes commitment and real, substantial dedication. Culture is lived through your people.

Culture manifests relationships within your pack. We show our care and compassion for our pack mates. We acknowledge and celebrate their strengths and differences. We understand our rights as a pack member while embracing our responsibilities to the pack. We value how our team plays the game. Our culture creates our team ethos.

All members of the pack are engaged in the process of co-constructing culture. It's an all-hands-on-deck proposition. This means added responsibility for the coach. The coach is ultimately responsible for how his team gets along, develops, and performs. Creating a sustainable and positive team culture is dynamic and a bit like cooking because you're adding and bringing the key ingredients of culture together at the right time. You're crafting the right recipe for your team.

Each of our teams will be unique and will require different leadership and coaching. Consistency is key when building culture. Stick with the basic ingredients. The following are the key ingredients of culture.

Culture's Key Ingredients

Authentic and real—The best version of you will bring out the best version in others. Members of the pack need to keep it real. This is especially true for coaching. Emulating other teams and leaders can be positive, but striving to create a carbon copy of another team's culture won't work. They are a different pack. Be your authentic self.

Co-learning—You are always learning and growing as a human being and so are your players. Embracing a growth mindset is imperative. You are modeling learning for your players and pack. Continuous learning means you are learning right alongside your players. Sharing this love of learning permits you to try to be 1 percent better today than you were yesterday.

Co-creating—Culture is living and being shaped by everyone in it. It's a shared responsibility. Players create it. Coaches create it. Parents create it. Ownership of the culture is cultivated through shared leadership and shared creation.

Standards and expectations—Culture is the way we do things around here. You strive to have high standards for your team. You have high expectations, inspiring others to raise their bar. Standards define the expected behaviors, attitudes, and beliefs of your pack members. These serve as our operating instructions by guiding and influencing individual and collective action.

Collaboration—This is key for your pack. The members of your pack need to serve each other: pack before self. Players need to compete for and with each other and not against. This is collaboration. The best in you brings out the best in us. We are all learning and growing together. A spirit of collaboration and service allows your players to be committed to a critical ideal of collaboration; that is, to be the best players *for* the team rather than the best players *on* the team.

Defining success—Success needs to be defined for your pack. This definition is unique from team to team. As we saw in chapter 2, you need to understand how you define success as a coach. This allows you to help your pack create a framework for winning and losing, moving your team beyond the lights and numbers on the scoreboard. The environment and spirit of your pack is shaped by your perspective on success. Your players play and compete for many different reasons. Their reasons need to be understood and celebrated because they will be various: aspiring to achieve personal bests and set records; learning how to play the game; learning teamwork. For some people it'll be learning to follow instructions while others will be focused on acquiring the character skills sport can teach. Success is what you want it to be. Why are we better for having played the game? Remember that it's the journey, not the destination.

Make mistakes—Sports and teams are a classroom, and mistakes are going to happen. Our efforts are not going to go our way every time. Perfection is not possible. What matters is our response to our mistakes. Create environments where mistakes are celebrated as learning opportunities. Make mistakes fast and move beyond them faster.

Responsibilities and rights—Being part of a pack is a privilege. This privilege comes with both rights and responsibilities. As we discussed in chapter 3, individuals have rights as members of the pack: the right to be respected, to feel safe, to experience the game at their level. These rights help your players feel appreciated and valued. Their rights as pack members are in concert with their responsibilities to the pack. The pack is greater than any single wolf. Our pack members are accountable to each other to honor everyone's rights while delivering on their responsibilities.

Person, Player, Performer—All your players were people before they joined your team, and they will be people long after. You are focused on the development of the whole person and not just the athlete. The person matters most of all. This is a holistic approach. "Center," "guard," "first baseman" describe athletes and performers but not people. Certainly teach sport skills but move beyond titles and labels. Develop the person first.

Buy-In—Ownership is developed through the process of co-creating your pack's standards and expectations. Ownership brings selective perception to your team. You all see things in the same way because you co-created it. For your team, sharing the same values, behaviors, and beliefs is critical to foster buy-in and commitment. Committed individuals work for the good of the pack. Accountability and responsibility to the pack flow directly from one's commitment.

Purpose—Our purpose needs to be clearly defined. Striving to win, sure. Striving to create a high-functioning and positive team, yes. But our purpose is much greater. It represents our *why*, and it is more intricate. Why are we coaching? What is our mission as a member of this pack? Our purpose needs to be bigger than wins and losses, trophies and medals. This distinction can be subtle and yet very important. A culture needs a clear purpose that is beyond winning and beyond the game. Our culture needs to be focused on aiding people in becoming the best version of themselves.

My pack will co-create its own unique values and ethics. We believe this, this, and this. Therefore we behave in this way. The application of cultural ingredients establishes our pack environment. Behavior strategies emerge from our need to actualize and live out our beliefs. Uncertainty of action is overcome through the use of strategies.

Consistently living out values is the goal for any high-functioning team. Let's examine some winning strategies for creating a positive team culture.

Winning Strategies

Good Coaches Enjoy Their Players and Enjoy the Game

You really can identify the good coach quickly. She is out there with the kids, enjoying them, enjoying the game. Her practices are fun to watch. As you watch, you are aware of the lack of stress. In place of stress is intensity: working hard on skills and strategies. There is a lot of activity, and you can see challenges being thrown out to the players, some fun competitions.

During the game he is intense. He has high expectations and demands focus and alertness from the players. He is always very positive, "Way to stand in there." "Nice catch." "Way to back up the catcher." "Good eye." He doesn't throw compliments around. When you get one, it means something and the players respond with energy and purpose. Sometimes he's appropriately demanding—"Where were you on that rundown? You need to help Paul out on that play"—but he is never demeaning, sarcastic, or insulting.

The calm, firm, positive coach is more effective and wins more games than the loud, abusive, hard-nosed coach. In his own way he is just as intense and a much stronger person. The best coaches have both high support and high challenge beliefs and behaviors.

Good Coaches Deal with the Whole Player

Good coaches are aware that their players are whole human beings. Besides being athletic persons, they are mental, social, emotional, esthetic, school, and family persons. There are times when other parts of their lives distract them and they just can't focus all their energy and attention on the game or on practice. We have to respect and honor the other parts of their lives and keep the game in perspective. Remember: In the final analysis, it's a game and only a game.

Good Coaches Set Behavior Goals with Their Players

It is common procedure for coaches to specify behavioral goals for their players; for example, how to take directions from the coaches, how to treat your teammates, how to deal with opponents talking, and on and on. It is thereby essential that coaches work with their players in setting these goals and, equally important, that they include their own behavior in the list. "Players, you don't use abusive language, and we coaches also will not use abusive language."

Good Coaches Create Respect for One Another

Positive coaches respect their players and therefore they're respected by their players. The goal is mutual respect. That is not the same message as "They may not like me, but they're going to respect me." Fear is not the same as respect. You get respect the hard way: you earn it.

Good Coaches Teach and Use Cooperation

Positive coaches believe in competition but that comes only after they have built up a great sense of cooperation. First you play with your teammates, and then you play against your opponents.

Good Coaches Coach with Positive Expectancy

Good coaches expect things to work out well and communicate this to their players. We get what we expect to get. If you expect Larry to give you trouble, you get it. If you expect Larry to be okay, you have a chance to be right.

Good Coaches Relate to Their Players' Needs

All of us have needs that must be attended to and fulfilled. Here are the needs of kids.

- self-identity and recognition
- belonging to a community (your team)
- power and input
- success experiences

- knowledge of their growth

Good Coaches Set Performance Goals with Their Players and Their Teams

Your players must have some input into their goals; they must have some ownership. They will work harder to attain their goals if they're involved in selecting them. Setting goals keeps us focused and helps us stay on course. If you don't set goals and know where you're going, you'll probably end up somewhere else.

Good Coaches Recognize Individual Uniqueness

One of the things that we are sure of is that each of us is a unique individual. We all want to be treated as something special.

Good Coaches Recognize Different Patterns of Behavior

There are patterns of behavior that all of us adopt in order to be able to deal with the world. Sometimes we want to reach a goal to accomplish something that is important to us. Sometimes we have to protect ourselves from pain or embarrassment. Sometimes we need to be noticed and affirmed by peers or adults. Sometimes we need to get away from other people or painful circumstances. Sometimes we need to be able to take control of some part of our lives.

To do that we are apt to become whiners or clowns or pests or whatever best suits our needs. A caring mentor or coach will help us find healthy, productive ways to reach our goals so that we won't need to play the games that hinder our growth and hurt our team effort.

THE TEAM WORKING AND PLAYING TOGETHER

Sometime in the future people will look at our culture and will find that the best examples of teamwork—group goal-setting and achievement—were in our team sports ventures. In team sports it is essential that we first have cooperation among all elements of the team in order to compete at a much higher level against our opponents. In team sports, cooperation always precedes competition.

Goals are organized plans that define the direction and the level of achievement that we hope to reach. They provide purpose for our activity and give it direction. Without goals our efforts tend to wander. We wouldn't think of beginning a long trip without first knowing where we planned to go. Likewise, we will plan our pack with a set of goals by which we can determine how far we have come and how far we still have to go. Goals keep us from going off our planned course.

Team Goal-Setting

Goals must be challenging, they must demand a great deal of effort and dedication on your part and on the part of your players. Unless your goals really challenge you and make you work, you won't improve, and you will not be any better for having reached them.

New and higher goals are set before you reach the old ones. When your team is well on its way to reaching one of your goals, set a new and higher goal. For example, if you set a goal for a winning season (8-6 would be a winning season) and you are now 6-3, set a higher standard: "We are going to make the playoffs." Reaching a goal without having a new one to go after is a good way to get stuck.

Goals must be realistic. If your team went 0-14 last year, it would be unrealistic for you to set a team goal of a 14-0 season. Study the abilities of your team carefully and discuss goals with your players. They can help you establish challenging but realistic goals.

The Process

This goal-setting process must be done early in the season. There are five steps in the process.

Step 1: Positive Expectancy. The coaches will enter into all of their activities with positive expectancy, the belief that the situation will work out the way they want it to.

Step 2: Co-Creating the Goals. Ask players and coaches to list their goals, including character goals and behavior goals. Include goals that everyone can subscribe to, such as "To have a winning season." The commitment is to list the goals and try to get total agreement on each of them. Total agreement on these goals unifies the team. If we allow doubt to enter our minds, the doubt becomes our expectancy.

Step 3: Affirmation of Goals. Write an affirmation of each of these goals. Rewrite the goals in positive terms using first-person plural (for the team) and present tense; for example, "We are a winning team, and we are having a very successful season."

Step 4: Motivating Your Players. Coaches can motivate their team in any of five basic ways. The first four are external systems. The last one is internal, coming from the player herself. We all have had experience with the first two, the stick and the carrot.

The *stick approach* is the use of fear, threats, and punishment to change the efforts or behavior of the player. "Fred, you didn't get a goal today. You could lose your position."

The *carrot approach* is "Anybody who gets two or more shots wins a sticker on her bag." This is based on what the coach wants. It is not necessarily in the best interest of the player.

The *reward system* is significantly different because the reward is given without the player asking for it or expecting it. Luis has had a good day on the track so you compliment him on this at the closing meeting of the day.

Inspiration is the fourth type of motivation. The coach and his assistants are always acting honestly and with a lot of class. They stay positive and inspire others to learn more, move outside their comfort zone, and perform at new levels.

Accomplishment is the fifth type of motivation and is internal. You remember Ms. Rinehart, don't you? She was that fantastic music teacher everyone loved. You did your best for her and also for yourself. It's an internal process and it belongs to your players. Internal motivation is what you want to create—everything else will work if you have this.

Step 5: Goals Achieved and Success. An excellent definition of success is the achievement of goals that you have set for yourself. As your players reach their personal goals, give them the recognition that they've earned: a written note, an emblem, a pat on the back, a comment during a debriefing meeting, a text or call to parents—whatever fits the situation. You must do that for yourself also—you deserve it.

Never Lose Sight of Your Major Goal

The realization of your ultimate goals will not come easily. As a result, it is critical that you always keep those major goals in sight. Never forget what you are striving for. If you lose sight of this, you will become less motivated and find yourself putting forth less effort than you should. It is easy to grow discouraged and give up unless you remember your dream and how good you will feel when it becomes a reality.

It is also easy to spend too much time looking back on your past successes before you have reached your major goal. Once you begin to feel satisfied with your achievements in the past, you lose sight of your objective. Never look back until you have reached all your goals.

5

COACHING PRACTICE

The gym is dark. The field is empty. The water in the swimming pool is as still as a sheet of glass. These venues are our classrooms. We eagerly await the arrival of our players for practice. Coaches are teachers, and teachers are coaches. A field, a kayak course, a swimming pool, and a bowling alley are our classrooms. This is where we coach and teach our players. Our fields become our classrooms.

Our privilege is to be able to develop our pack both as people and as sportspeople. Coaches have the responsibility to teach many important life lessons in addition to the skills and strategies of their sport. Our culture and learning environment roar to life on our practice field.

Sport is what draws our pack together. How positively and productively we function, learn, and grow is what keeps us together. Players show up not as empty vessels to be filled but as wonderful people with their own unique ideas to express and their yet-undiscovered talents.

Practice needs to create an enriching and exciting learning environment for players. Engage and grab your players' attention. Allow them to joyfully experience and discover the game. Give them a platform and environment where they can make decisions and develop their skills and techniques. They want to play their game.

Learning new things and developing new habits can be challenging. Our current unconscious habits make us feel safe and secure. It's what we know how to do. During our practices, we are going to help our players get outside their comfort zone. We want them to learn new skills and implement newly found strategies. Collaborating, we are going to form new habits.

Some of us have played the sports that we coach and some of us haven't. Some of us know all the skills and strategies of that sport. Some of us don't. No matter our background, one of our primary responsibilities as coaches is to co-create a positive practice and learning environment for our players. Setting up this type of sports classroom means appreciating how our players are going to best learn and develop new skills and habits. We are moving beyond Xs and Os and truly earning the title "Coach."

PSYCHOLOGY AND LEARNING

Learning is much more than changing what we do. In order to really learn something, we must change our feelings and thoughts about and perceptions of what we are learning. Gail may decide to learn how to hit a right-to-left draw off the tee so she can add a few yards to her drives. In order to do that, she must change her thoughts about her total game. She has been hitting a left-to-right fade for all her golfing life. Now she has to change her visualizing process, her placement for her next shot, and her picture of what a good drive looks like. When we teach our players something new or are installing different habits, we're changing a number of things and we have to be patient while the changes take place.

Basic Performance Modes

There are two different performance modes in sport: practice mode and game mode. Each mode has unique and important characteristics. Understanding these modes allows us to appropriately turn them on for our players.

Practices are different from games and particularly for players more than eight years old. Practices take place in a sports classroom. Players learn new skills and strategies there. Playing modified games and activities enhances decision making and development of adaptable skills. Mistakes and errors are expected. Team practices are enriching learning environments. Our players are developing new habits.

Games are played on ball fields, courts, courses. These are the players' stage. Our players are performing in the arena. Games feel different. Games contain elements that aren't present in practice mode such as uniforms, parents, opponents, officials, scoreboards, lights, and so forth. There is the pressure to perform and help determine the result. We must help and guide our players through the experience of competing in games.

Switching between modes is much like playing a video game. Your players will understand the difference. Use this analogy and terminology with them. Operating effectively in each mode improves their learning and experience.

Practice Mode

The purpose of practice mode is to allow players to learn new skills and mechanics and to sharpen up the ones they have already learned. You can teach the skills and shorten Jessica's stride so she won't strike out so much; you can teach Gary how to make the outlet pass on a fast break. You can teach your players the infield fly rule, the difference between a corner kick and goal kick, what icing is, or leg before wicket. You can teach your players the strategies that will be used in the games: infielders running down a runner, blitzing on third down, a full court press, when the fly half kicks the ball.

Practice mode is for an individual player to improve on a skill to the point that she will be able to perform it when the time comes for the use of that skill. Standing at the free throw line in the big game is not the time to adjust your shooting rhythm. That kind of experimenting must be done in practice.

Likewise, it simply doesn't make any sense to use a new tactic in game mode that your players haven't had some experience with in practice mode. Players need to be able to discover and work through the elements of a new tactic. Understanding the ins and outs of a tactic or strategy helps to make it at least to some degree automatic.

Game Mode

You have to trust what you have learned in practice mode and then do it. The key word is "trust"—no second guessing. Sam Snead was once asked what he thought about as he was addressing the ball and he said, "If I thought about anything, I would probably miss the darn ball."

The skills and strategies on display during game mode are developed and encoded during the discovery and creative stages of practice mode. No two laps or passes are exactly alike. Similar qualities? Yes. Exactly the same? No. Game mode brings out new scenarios.

Deliberate practice gives players an adaptable skill set to apply in game mode. Players have developed their game. They trust it! Trust brings confidence. And confidence increases enjoyment and execution for players. When you have learned a new skill in practice mode, you must trust yourself and use it without fear in game mode.

Good coaches use both a reinforcement model and an awareness model so that their players will learn their skills until they become automatic.

Habits

Habits control 80 to 90 percent of our daily operations. Habits include such activities as brushing our teeth. They keep us safe, on task, and alive. Often these habits are created without our knowledge. Our subconscious habits have been formed and ingrained over the years through our response to the various circumstances and challenges in life. These habits allow us to act without thinking. The same thing is true in our playing sports. We need to act without thinking, to act instinctively or automatically or by habit most of the time. We need to program our game so that we make the right moves in action while we're using our mind to deal with the current situation.

What we do in coaching is move action (physical movement and skill) and thinking (awareness and strategy) from the conscious to the subconscious mind so that we can improve performance on the field. To put it simply, we try to have our players get into the habit of doing the right things on the field. We want them to tag second base while going from first to third without thinking, "I have to tag second base." That skill should have been burned into the player's operation so that he can concentrate on picking up the signs from the third-base coach. There are three facets of habit forming to deal with here.

1. Establishing new habits (learning)
2. Extinguishing old unwanted habits (unlearning)
3. Replacing old habits with new ones (relearning)

Establishing New Habits

Working with young players on the co-ed softball team, Falcons head coach Marianne Ames and assistant coaches Sara Garcia and Glen Tracy are mainly concerned with establishing new habits. Fred Johnson came to the Falcons with no playing experience. When Coach Garcia works with him on fielding a ground ball in the outfield, she can go directly to showing him how to hurry to get in front of the ball, to get into the correct fielding position, to have his glove in the correct position, and so on. This is relatively easy because there are no old habits to unlearn as the new ones are acquired. Fred is not doing anything that needs to be changed.

However, it is essential that Fred is not seen as coming to the team with no information about or experience with this skill. Throughout his young life, Fred has stopped a rolling ball with his foot or hand. He simply has not used a lot of his life actions to focus on that specific action as it is used in this game.

You have to be careful here, so here is an urgent warning. It is essential that you teach Fred the correct way to do things: the simplest way but also the correct way *for Fred*. Yes, the correct way for Fred. Not the vision for the skill that you have in your head or the skill as it is pictured in *101 Greatest Sports Drills*.

We need to teach the characteristics of the skill to fit each player. The player has to see it and feel it. Skillful performers adapt their skills to solve problems presented in their game. *This means players are playing the game versus performing the skill.* If we make the learning a habit just for the time being, we will have to make the player unlearn it and relearn a new correct way to do it at a later time.

Learning the Right Way: A Lesson from a Thinking Coach

Retired coach Larry Watson noticed while watching Tee-ball games that these new batters were hitting the ball into the ground near the plate rather than out to the field. He commented on that to Ralph, a friend of his and the parent of a player on one of the teams he had been watching. That started a discussion on how the players had been told to hit the ball. It seems that they were simply told to look at the back of the ball and then hit it. When they did that they would take the bat down from their shoulder and hit the ball above the center line and the ball would go into the ground.

"So what can we do about that?" Ralph asked Larry.

"Well, a good batter is always looking out to where he wants to hit the ball. So next practice, have some coaches and players out in the field. Tell the batters to look out there and hit the ball to those people out there." Coach Larry demonstrated how that would change their stance and the path of the bat. The bat would hit the ball at a lower spot and send it to a better place.

The next time Ralph and Larry got together, Ralph told him that the kids' hitting was greatly improved. The kids were dropping into a hitting stance and swinging more freely, and the balls were going off the tee and out to the field. In fact, they'd won their last game. The coffee that morning was on Ralph.

Extinguishing Old Habits

Extinguishing old habits can be a bigger problem because someone is asked to create a vacuum in his or her behavior, and vacuums invite old behaviors to come back. Someone we know had an experience with this when he left Langston University and took a position at the University of Oklahoma. In getting to Langston University, he used to travel north on I-35 and get off at the Guthrie exit. Several months later, he was going north on I-35 to a conference in Stillwater, which is a good distance north of Guthrie.

Well, you know what happened. There he was on the off-ramp at the Guthrie exit. He just laughed (there are times that we simply must laugh at ourselves), crossed over to the on-ramp to I-35, and continued on his way. The next time he traveled that way, he filled the vacuum by giving himself a verbal and visual cue and kept going north on I-35.

There are times you lose a skill because of a physical loss. On the par five number 7 hole, you can't clear that lake with a driver off the tee any longer so you take out your newly purchased hybrid club and hit a shot that doesn't reach the water—a lay-up. You have essentially given up your chances for a birdie and are now playing for a par.

Sometimes there's a rule change that affects your behavior. In some men's slow-pitch softball leagues there were too many home runs, so a limit on home runs (e.g., three home runs per game) was established.

The home run specialists had to change their high fly ball over the fence, which would now be an out, to a low line drive or grounder.

Replacing Old Habits with New Habits

Connie's case is much tougher. She has been coached by her parents from year one and she has acquired some softball habits that are keeping her from improving. Her dad wanted her to be a pitcher (what else?) so she would be the star. He had been a good baseball player but he knew nothing about softball pitching. Connie learned a lot of poor habits. especially in coordinating her arm swing with her stride. Head Coach Ames has her playing third base while Coach Garcia gives her pitching instruction. In this case, Connie has to replace old, ingrained habits with new ones, and the tendency to revert to the old ways when there's a critical situation.

When Coach Garcia has Connie pretty well coordinated on the mound, Coach Ames decides to let her start a game at pitcher. She is doing pretty well but in the third inning after an error in the infield and losing a hitter on a pretty good 3-and-2 pitch, she loses her cool and throws four balls to the next batter that don't come near the strike zone.

Coach Garcia jumps up in the dugout and says to Coach Ames, "Get her out of there." Coach Ames says, "What did you see?" "She's back to her old arm swing and stride. She won't get another pitch over the plate." Coach Ames, having confidence in her assistant coach, goes out and makes the change.

When things went astray, Connie subconsciously reverted to her old, tried-and-trusted pitching style. This is often called the comfort zone. Next practice, Coach Garcia will be working again with Connie in practice mode until Connie is really ready to trust her new pitching style and skills enough to stay with them in game mode.

We tend to revert to our old and comfortable ways when a situation gets critical.

Behavioral Habits

Coach Roberts is concerned by the behavior of Carl (the Clown). One of Carl's favorite antics is getting his teammate's attention as he steps into the batter's box and trying to make him laugh with funny faces, funny names, or funny actions. It is fun and he gets a lot of positive feedback from the players who laugh along with him, but it is distracting to the player who is trying to concentrate—to get the sign—to be ready for the pitch. Let's listen in as Coach Roberts deals with this one.

Coach: Carl, what are you doing?

Carl: I'm helping take the pressure off Benny. He's too uptight.

Coach: When you're getting ready to bat, you close your eyes and do some deep breathing.

Carl: Yeah, Coach Davis has been showing us how to focus better.

Coach: And how does it work for you?

Carl: It's great. I'm hitting a lot better now.

Coach: Now tell me how making Benny laugh helps him to focus.

Carl: Hmm. I never thought about that. But I've always done this fun stuff.

Coach: I know, and you really help all of us enjoy the game more. But is this the right time to do that with Benny?

Carl: I guess not . . . but I'm so used to doing things.

Coach: Will you do this for your teammates? Just ask yourself this question when you're having fun: How is this helping Benny and helping the team?

Carl: Okay, it's a deal. And I suppose you'll remind me.

Coach: Of course. That's what coaches do.

Good habit change is not focused on what you did wrong, it deals with what you're going to do to make it right.

THE SUPER SEVEN STRATEGIES

The super seven strategies are used by coaches and teachers to help their kids learn faster and play better.

Primacy: The first time you learn something is very important.

Recency: The most recent time that you've learned something is very important.

Repetition: Practice correctly to improve performance.

Reinforcement: Use the basic reward system to maintain your progress.

Awareness: Know and use the whole picture.

Achievement: Reach the goals that you set for yourself.

Closure: Complete tasks so that you can move on to new ones.

If these strategies are not separated from one other, they'll flow together in a very natural way. You should be asking the player to be aware of the situation (achievement) and then use closure so his brain has time to deal with it before you move on to another issue.

Though we have many techniques at our disposal to form habits, we will focus on these seven habit-forming strategies. None of these is better than the others. Each of them is simply more appropriate relative to the learner and to the skills or knowledge that are to be learned. You don't teach your seven-year-olds the full-court zone press regardless of how good a coach you are and how great a command you have of your coaching skills. In like manner, you don't walk a college-level player around the bases so that she knows you go from first to second to third and third to home. Yes, you might have advanced players that you sometimes feel must be taken back to that level. You may have read that at the first practice after a poor game by the Green Bay Packers, Coach Vince Lombardi held up a football and said, "This is a football."

Players come to play with a lot of experiences that are related to the game. Now they will be learning how to use those as skills in new ways. During this teaching and learning time, you want your players to be adept at and comfortable with their skill and strategies in practice mode. We must meet each player exactly where he is and help him improve his performance.

Primacy: The First Time You Learn Something Is Very Important

It is essential the first time you introduce a new skill or activity that you teach it correctly and significantly. This is the time you set the base for its use, and all of the times the player uses it thereafter, he will be building on this base. You will have great problems in the future if you must change the way the player first encountered a skill. When a coach says, "This is the way they will learn it right now. Later we will change it to a better way," he is asking for trouble. Later it will require unlearning and relearning.

Coach Tracy is working with his pitchers. "We have told you that besides pitching a ball, you have to be a defensive player. Today we will work on balls that are hit toward the right side of the field. As soon as a ball is hit to the second baseman, the first baseman, or to the hole between them, you are going to take off toward first base. I will be in the batter's box. You will make the usual kind of pitch and I will hit a ball somewhere on the right side. When you see the ball going to that side, take off full speed. The fielders will do their job."

With that explanation made, Coach Tracy starts the drill with easy grounders and later harder grounders to the right side of the field— always commenting on the performances of the players. When he has made a lot of comments such as "That's the way," he calls the pitchers together and gives them some feedback.

It is important that the first experiences in a practice session are successful ones. That's why we warm up with easy grounders and then build up to tough ones. If we start out hitting scorchers, the players will have pretty poor experiences to build on. In this session, the players had successful attempts on their last attempts. Coach Tracy reinforced their good attempts with verbal rewards and sent the satisfied players on to their next task.

It is important to use this strategy without the learner being aware of its use. Every salesperson knows that he must make a great first impression. And you may be sure that he will have you smiling when you leave. Movie people grab you right at the start and then send you home with something to keep in your memory. They want you to remember it so well that you'll tell your friends about this good movie.

Notice that in this discussion of primacy we have inevitably moved into some examples of recency. Observe that much of the time when we say "last," we really mean "latest." For example, you might say, "The last time I swam 1,500 meters, I swam pretty well," but it is understood that you really intend to swim many more 1,500-meter races before you swim your last.

Recency: The Most-Recent Time You've Learned Something Is Very Important

In the practice session on covering first base, the players took successful attempts away with them. Coach Tracy reinforced their good attempts with verbal rewards and sent the satisfied players on to their next task. We store away the final part of an experience with our feelings. Feelings are more important than thoughts here. The feelings we carry away from an experience are very strong and they significantly reinforce our thoughts.

Here's another sports example. In tennis you want your players to start off hitting easy serves and build up from there, letting the rhythm become ingrained. Joyce has been hitting good practice serves and she has just stroked a beauty. Coach Bruce anchors this by saying, "Fantastic, get over with the folks working on their backhands." Success breeds success.

The most-recent time you have worked with your players is the one you want them to keep and use. This is the one you have been working toward with your players, and this is the one you want to reinforce.

Repetition: Practice Correctly to Improve Performance

Coach Garcia is out in center field helping Paula with catching flies and throwing directly to the plate. She noticed last game that Paula caught a fly ball flat footed and threw too late to catch the runner on third, who tagged up and scored. Coach Garcia has a parent, Geno Pacetti, hitting nice, soft fly balls into short center field, and she is demonstrating how to set up a couple of steps back and then move in to catch the ball and throw in one fluid motion. She is verbally describing what she's doing, and she is asking Paula to verbalize what she's seeing.

Now Coach Garcia has Paula doing dry runs, moving forward and pretending to catch the ball and throwing to the plate. After five attempts, Coach Garcia sees what she wants, a really good attempt, so she anchors it. "Looks good, Paula. Now let's take some real flies." Geno hits more flies and Paula handles them all very well. Coach Garcia taps Paula on the shoulder and says, "Good work. Now walk back to the fence and take a few minutes to think about what you just did and get into good feelings about it—like that smile you had when you caught that last one and threw a one-hop strike to the plate."

Coach Garcia made sure that Paula handled the task well at the close. Then she gave her an anchor, a verbal reward on her most recent attempt, and the time and space to do a full visualization using sensory memory and positive feelings.

Here's a non-sports example. Fourth-grade children learning to spell new words are told by Mr. Shepherd to write each word twenty times (Did you hear the groans?). This practice is called a drill. Mr. Shepherd noted that after the students had made about five good attempts the quality of the writing started going down, and by the fifteenth attempt the words were either misspelled or illegible or both. This meant that the last words they wrote, whose images were sent to their memory bank (recency), were interfering with their ability to spell those words correctly. So Mr. Shepherd got smart, and his kids got happy. He told them to write each word five times and really focus on each one. As a result, they wrote very neat papers because their first and most-recent attempts (primacy and recency) were excellent models to store in visual and kinesthetic memory.

The younger the player, the sooner she becomes bored with or just plain tired of repetitive actions. When your kids are practicing, they must be as focused as they are in a game. Practice does not make perfect, practice makes semipermanent or permanent.

At a practice session, Sam is at the foul line getting in the last few of his twenty-five shots and all he's doing is throwing the ball up there and Herb and Jason are rebounding his shots and having fun with the ball before getting it back to him.

This activity is not non-productive, it's counterproductive. Sam is actually practicing poor shooting, and he will probably get very good at poor shooting because he is internalizing bad habits that will be present when a game situation is at hand. Practice creates stability, and if Sam isn't careful, bad foul shooting will become a default condition. Every practice shot has to be made as if the player's in a real competitive situation. Sam must go through all the steps on each practice shot so that in the game his subconscious mind will take over and he will be operating in performance mode. And his partners have to help him.

The need to practice skills by repetition is critical in all sports, but practice is different for different people. It makes sense to have a standard, reasonable number of reps and then let those who want more help themselves. Knowing when to stop practicing a skill is just as important as getting started: "Okay, one more serve as good as the last one and we'll start on your forehand." A few focused attempts are much better than many unfocused attempts.

Reinforcement: Use the Basic Reward System to Maintain Your Progress

At the crack of the bat, Coach Ames groans. A sharply hit liner flashes through the hole between first and second. "Oh no, that'll bring in two runs." But not yet. Alexis charges in from short right field, picks up the ball on first bounce, and throws a strike to Connie, who has come over from the pitcher's box to cover first. "You're out!" calls Umpire Jake Abrams. "That's three outs—let's go, in and out." The first one to reach Alexis as she comes in off the field is Coach Ames, with a high five and "Great play! Fantastic throw!" She then high-fives Connie, saying, "Heads up play! That's the way to cover first base!"

The sooner you tie the reinforcement to the incident, the stronger it is. Coach Ames did it right. However, there is another good way to do it. After Alexis and Connie get the good stuff from their teammates and Coach Ames, Coach Garcia, who has been working with Alexis, sits down with her and says, "You just made all the hard work you did in practice pay off. That was a terrific play—you are getting to be a terrific asset to our team."

Coach Garcia did three things and did them well. First, she gave Alexis a verbal reward for her actions just as the other coaches and players had. Second, this reward would have been less intense than the others because of the time lapse between the incident and the response but she made up for that by giving her comments more intensity and by tying it to Alexis's work in practice. Third, in addition to reinforcing what she did, she reinforced Alexis for who she is as a person. The reinforcement model is very simple to use—in fact, we all use it frequently. We use it with our children, our pets, our employees, our friends. We most often don't realize that we're using it. We also most often use it honestly. Often we reinforce people for what they do but we forget to reinforce and appreciate them for who they are.

Watch the dog whisperer. He has a message for coaches too. If you want your dog to learn the command "Sit up," you say, "Sit," you sit him up, then you say, "Good dog," and you give him a dog snack. Eventually when you say "Sit," the dog sits and you give him another verbal reward and snack. If he doesn't sit, you very patiently go over it again. You don't yell, "You stupid dog, what's wrong with you? Can't you learn anything?"

But there is also negative use of reinforcement. There is an old story about a prospector in the Old West who struck a mother lode. He was headed back East with his young son and several bags full of gold nuggets. He wanted his son to remember where the gold mine was so he stopped his wagon at several landmarks. He told his son to look at those landmarks as he spanked the dickens out of him so he would never forget them. Of course that's not what happened. Instead, his son stored all that information way back in his data banks with the other bad experiences that he wanted to forget.

What happens to your pitcher when all you do is yell at him for not backing up the catcher on a throw to the plate from the left fielder? What happens to your relay anchor leg when all you do is shout at her for not starting correctly and taking off too soon? These are experiences that they are ready to forget. And what they forget will include what you may have told them to do to improve their performance. That is what you wanted to reinforce.

Awareness: Know and Use the Whole Picture

The liner ricocheted off Tim's glove at first base and bounced toward center field. Tim took off after it and ran it down. Terry, the catcher, had to stay home because of the runner on second going to third and Connie, the pitcher, was backing him up. Tim picked up the ball and saw that the batter had rounded first and come down the line toward second. As Tim looked toward first, he saw that Alexis had come in from right field to help out. The runner turned to go back just in time to see Alexis waiting for the throw from Tim. Good throw, runner's out. All of the reinforcement tactics were joined with the appropriate awareness here.

How can you teach that? Alexis saw the whole picture: she saw where she might be needed and she got there. Some people seem to have it and others never seem to get it. A lot of our problems are the result of teaching the kids the game in a very narrow way. On the Herons basketball team, Curt is a guard and his coaches teach him all the guard stuff. He has no idea what the center does, and the center has no idea what the guard does. Neither one of them knows what the forwards do, and so forth. It is important for each of your players to experience what each of his teammates is doing, so during basketball practices, for example, have the guards play center for a while, the forwards play guard, the centers play forward, and so on. They soon will know what their teammates have to deal with, creating better team-work.

Let's talk about context. Sometimes too much time is spent teaching skills and practicing with many repetitions that are separate from real game conditions. This results in having an experience so far removed from game conditions that the practice may not be relevant. One answer is to do a lot of simulated practice with the whole team involved. Make the plays real. "Okay, guys, one out, runner on second" (and there is a real runner on second). You hit a fly ball to right center. The second baseman goes out for a possible relay, the shortstop covers second, the third baseman covers third, the center fielder is catching the ball, and the right fielder is backing him up. That's it? Of course not. The other players are also learning their tasks.

Ask this question a lot: What could you have done on that play that might have helped? In the example at the start of this section, Alexis could have seen the play as very simple. The ball wasn't hit to her so there was nothing for her to do on this play. She could just go back to her right field position and get ready for the next pitch. But she knew better.

Here's the bottom line: whatever your sport is, you have to teach your players all of the rules, all of the tactics, all of the operations of the game. Sometimes it's on the practice field, sometimes it's on the chalkboard, sometimes it's on the bench, sometimes it's on the playing field, sometimes it's on the clipboard—but it's always there to do.

Achievement: Reach the Goals That You Set for Yourself

We're at an end-of-the-season award banquet and we see Coach Hall of the Tigers handing the Sportsmanship Award trophy to Colby, a member of his team. Terry Simmons of our Falcons will be accepting the Most Valuable Player Award from Coach Ames.

There will be winners and there will be losers. So how do we separate the sheep from the goats? Let's put this in broader terms. Who determines whether you are a winner or a loser? Can you decide if someone else is a winner or a loser? How much do we allow others to judge whether we are successful and how much judging of others do we do? And then there's the biggest question of all: after you decide who the losers are, what do you do with them?

Everyone on the team must believe that he is a winner—including the batboy. If you make any of them losers, you diminish the whole team. *Success is being where you are after you've done your very best.*

What you do and who you are are two different things. You can lose and not be a loser. You can be, act, and feel like a winner regardless of the circumstances. And when you do your very best, you are always a winner. And so it is with your team. The players, the parents, your assistant coaches, and you must all feel that you are winners. Love you for who you are and for what you do.

Closure: Complete Tasks So You Can Move On to New Ones

Coach Roberts has just completed a field session on backing up throws with his group. The kids are sitting on the bench in the third base dugout. "Okay, let's review this. Where does the pitcher go when . . . ?" This goes on until "Okay, folks, now let's get some batting practice in."

Coach Roberts has closed one task so that he and the players can go on to the next task. He really is clear that unless there is an urgent question, they are on the move. When we complete one lesson, it gives us the space to move on to the next one.

Here's a non-sports example. Jerry was painting his living room in a soft blue color his wife really liked but he ran out of paint a few feet left of one corner. Being very resourceful, he moved one of their end tables in front of it so no one could see the unfinished work.

But Jerry knows it's there, and every time he walks into that room his little mental reminder program says, "You've got to finish that paint job one of these days." After about a dozen of these episodes, Jerry goes to the store, buys a small can of the same paint, and completes the job: closure. Now he can walk into that room without being bugged by his brain.

And here's another sports example: Coach Ames is having a late dinner with her family and she is telling them about the really good practice session they had late that afternoon. She is in the middle of telling them about their new player when she exclaims, "Oh no! I knew all the way driving home that I had missed doing something, and I was kicking myself for not being able to remember what it was. Now I remember."

Her husband, Dan, says, "Okay, start at the beginning and tell us about it."

"Aki and his family just moved here from China. His father is American and his mother is Chinese. He's a good athlete but he needs some help. Tim Lindstrom, our present first baseman, took him under his wing today. He's helping him with our drills and with how the whole game is played. Tim simply made him a new friend and teammate. I forgot to thank Tim for what he's doing with Aki."

"Well, Mar, I think you can do it even better now. We know enough about the Lindstroms to share this with more than just Tim. After dinner, give his parents a call and tell them about this and also thank Tim the way you wanted to do."

Marianne's teen-age son, Jason, pipes up, "That sounds good to me too." Later that evening, Marianne talks to Elsa Lindstrom for a while and then thanks Tim personally for what he's been doing. I will leave you to think about all the future thoughts, feelings, and actions that may result from this short episode.

When your mind keeps bugging you, it often means that you didn't complete something. Complete it so you can move on.

CONFLICT RESOLUTION

The entire concept of conflict resolution is based on closure. At the beginning of this chapter Coach Roberts was really concerned about how Carl the Clown used his antics when they were inappropriate. How did they come to some resolution? Instead of sitting on it and being bent out of shape, Coach Roberts operated in such a way that he got closure on the issue. This closure enabled both Coach Roberts and Carl to move forward with their team goals. It ain't over 'til it's over—and then *it's over*!

Clearing Up Our Messages: It's Easy

Our messages matter to our players. What we say and how we say it can have a profound impact. So be clear. Be concise and say what you mean.

Evelyn is having trouble shooting with her laces, and you say, "It's easy. Just go ahead and do it." Sounds good to you, right? But what sounds right to you may be really bad for Evelyn. Let's get into her cleats.

If she doesn't begin doing it right, she might say to herself, "Coach said it was easy and I can't do it. I must be a pretty poor player."

If she finally gets it right, she may say to herself, "Well, I did it, but Coach said it was easy so it's no big deal."

So, Coach, you say this instead: "Shooting with your laces really is pretty hard but I know you will work hard on it and you will get it."

So now if she still doesn't get it right, she can say to herself, "Well, Coach said it's hard and I will keep working on it until I get it."

If she does manage to attain that skill, she can say to herself (and to anyone else in the area including you and her parents), "I got it!"

How many times have you had a player, such as Harry, say, "I don't know how to do this" and then just stand there waiting for you to do something? So you jump in and say, "Let me show you again." This encourages dependency (a red light).

Instead you say, "Well, Harry, show me what you can do" (a green light).

"Well, I can do this," he says, and he shows you what he can do. This gives you a place to start and move him on.

The main thing here is that you continue with the communication. But "All the other guys can do it" is not the way to continue the communication. Neither is "I've shown you how to do it a dozen times already." Both these exchanges create red lights.

Never help children do something they can do themselves. That is called enabling. Create green light moments with your communication.

Do You Speak a Foreign Language Such as Sportsese?

Sometimes coaches, in communicating with young players, will use sports terms, for example "Back up the catcher." We like to throw around sports jargon and other terms that show off our knowledge. And even though our players might not understand what we're saying, they'll nod their heads so they don't look like they don't know.

Age- and level-appropriate terms help with processing and comprehension. When you use understandable terms, your players will feel more secure and will perform with less stress. Encourage your players to speak up if they don't understand or need some clarification. And ask the right questions.

Coaches at times can do a lot of telling and not a lot of asking. And often the questions they ask don't do what they intended them to do. Let's start out with the wrong question. Ted has just struck out going after a bad pitch. Ted comes off the field and throws his bat on the ground. So you say to him, "Ted, why did you throw your bat on the ground?" (a red light). Ted answers, thinking he's about to get into trouble, "I don't know." This isn't a bad answer and it's very common. "Why did you?" questions are confrontational and invite a defensive response.

So instead you say to him, "Ted, what do you do with your bat when you're not using it?"

"I put it on the rack." (He knows he did something wrong.) "Okay, will you do that now?"

There was no argument—Ted gave you the correct answer himself. Now he is completing the task. Kids know to be careful when answering a question dealing with what they were supposed to do so they say, "I don't know." They get practice on this at home: "Why did you leave your dirty uniform in the kitchen?" "I don't know." Let's try it a different way: "Len, where's the right place to put your dirty uniform?" This is a green light, and Len not only knows the answer but he will give it to you. "I should have put it in the laundry room." "Okay, so will you do that now? That's great." Kids know how to do things in the appropriate and right ways. Just ask them the right question.

Inquiry Coaching and Interaction

Sandy is a new player on Coach Haley's junior high school basketball team. He has a lot of ability and has had very little coaching. He is now an eighth grader, and he started playing basketball team sports as a seventh grader. Coach Haley noticed that Sandy had trouble guarding a very good opponent in the game last week. It is now the first practice session after that game.

Coach Haley: Okay, Sandy, let's talk about guarding your man. Last game, your man drove around you a couple of times and you got a little frustrated. What was happening?

Sandy: He was too fast and I didn't have time to react before he got past me.

Coach: Right, so what could you have done about that?

Sandy: I don't know. I was in good position with him when he didn't have the ball but when he got the ball I couldn't stay with him.

Coach: Well, we were playing a tight man-to-man defense and you were really playing in his jersey. What could you have done?

Sandy: I think I see what you're getting to. When he got the ball, I could have moved off him a little and I would have had more time to react.

Coach: Right, you are pretty quick yourself but you give up that advantage when you try to guard anybody too close. Give yourself a little more space and trust your quick feet. Want to try it out?

Sandy: Yeah, I sure do.

Coach: Fred's our quickest driver. Hey, Fred, I want you to play a little one-on-one with Sandy here and I'll even let you have the ball all of the time. Okay, Sandy, check out what you have come up with and I'll keep an eye on you for a while.

Sandy: Okay, Coach! Let's *go*!

Note that Coach Haley asked Sandy three times what he could have done about the problem and led him to a good solution. And then he had him check it out in a real situation. If Sandy didn't find the solution by the third ask, Coach Haley could have nudged him by saying something like, "How tight were you playing him?"

Some coaches actually feel threatened when a player asks a question or even tries to discuss things with them, and they are apt to cut him off at the knees. Of course, that's the last time that player will ask a question, and the coach will be heard to say, "These kids never talk to me. They're not even interested enough to ask me what to do if they're not sure how to do it."

The smart coach knows that his players will learn faster and better if they are involved in the planning and execution of the learning process.

Remember to ask what or how questions instead of why questions: "What's the right way to do this?" or "How could you do this next time?" And listen to their response.

Praise and Encouragement

Often you will hear coaches say, "You have to praise your kids" or "We don't praise our kids enough." This can be a trap for both coach and player.

Coaches like to acknowledge kids for their efforts, but sometimes they send the wrong or an inadequate message. Shawna has just done a good job in practice passing the soccer ball to a teammate. So you say, "Great, that's the way to do it." That's praise—a yellow light. One message that Shawna gets is that she has reached a good level of passing the ball, and this has placed a mark on the level that you will accept and expect in the future. She doesn't have to do it any better.

So let's go one more step: "Terrific job. That was a big improvement. Now, next time you will want to want to give Debbie a little more lead because she's very fast." That's encouragement—a green light. Now you have covered both bases. You have told Shawna that she did something well and you have also told her how to improve on this skill. This is also a way of telling her what level of performance she will have to attain in order to get any more acknowledgment.

Praise and encouragement together are a great team for moving your people along.

Setting Up Our Practice

Practice is our sports classroom, our home base for learning and exploration where players (and coaches) discover their games and develop solutions to the challenges presented. The primary obstacles, the problem solving, and the success for players should be the game itself. The game is the canvas on which learning takes place.

One of our primary responsibilities as coaches is to co-create a productive practice environment. Intentionally and deliberately setting up an athlete-centered practice environment leads directly to enhanced player learning and enjoyment.

The Natural Way Is the Best Way

It is necessary to have your basketball players dribble, shoot, pass, and so forth as naturally for them as possible. In addition, there are things they can be told that will fit their mode and improve them. Coaches often interfere with the natural movements that their kids have so that they can give them the "right" moves.

Fran, the star pitcher on a semi-pro baseball team, had a natural sidearm delivery that was very effective for him and bad news for the opposing batters. He was picked up by a traveling squad in a larger city, and his new coach thought that Fran would be faster and more consistent if he threw three quarters. Well, you know what happened. Fran not only was less effective, he started to have pain in his pitching arm. This story has a happy ending. Fran got home and went back to his natural rhythm, and his pain left and his fastball and curve came back. If it ain't broke, don't fix it.

A bit of insight is required to create practices that best serve players. We need to be intentional about capturing elements of the natural way.

Our set-up needs to be purposeful as we strive to capture elements of the natural way as often as possible.

There is a real beauty in kids playing and experiencing their sport. A group of kids on a cold winter day playing pond hockey, for example; a hot afternoon with the sun beating down on a quick game of playground basketball; a crisp fall afternoon that brings out a game of street football with the goal line marked by a fire hydrant; or the long days of summer with kids of all ages running into the sandlot behind the grocery store for a game of stickball.

It is important to recognize what these sports moments share. These are the elements that we're deliberately trying to re-create during our practices. There is real joy. Everyone plays. There is fun in moving, learning, growing, and competing. Players try out and develop new skills. Players make decisions and think strategically. Creative thinking is the norm. Players engage their imagination and emulate their heroes. Rules are created and enforced. Rules keep things fair and fun!

Most importantly, playing the game is the focus. It is serious business. The kids want to keep playing even if that means moving under a streetlight as darkness descends or continuing the game tomorrow.

Do you notice what's missing from these neighborhood games? Think about it for a second. We aren't there. There are no coaches, no parents. The increased organization and structure in youth sport has often brought a more coach-centric view of practice in which it's assumed that players need to be told and instructed, need to be programmed with strategic decisions and drilled on the skills, need to attend practices filled with a coach's voice and structures.

Our players have wonderful yet undiscovered talents and skills. They have solutions to problems that we as coaches often don't see. Our practices need to engage their minds and their spirits. These players are partners and co-creators of the practice environment. This is where the magic of learning happens. Let's briefly explore how to capture the natural way and discuss best practice concepts to help us set up our next-level practices.

A Games-Based Approach

A long-standing myth in coaching is that skill mastery must come before playing the game. This traditional approach holds that techniques need to be learned apart from the tactics and strategy of a real game. Skills and techniques are often practiced in overly simplified situations or drills that do not simulate a real game. Players must be able to perform the drill before earning the opportunity to play the game.

This myth is deeply embedded in coaching culture. Perhaps it connects back to how we were coached or how we experienced physical education classes. A deep self-reflection dive is not required. Awareness of our unconscious belief about learning skills is imperative. We need to move beyond this traditional coaching myth.

A games-based approach is a better alternative approach to mindless drills during practice. In the games-based approach, there is a recognition of the connection between technique and strategy. Since players use both at the same time during games, we need to teach both at the same time during practice.

Techniques and strategies are both solutions to the problems and challenges presented within any game. For example, executing a quick free-kick in the middle third of the field. Just as you never step in the same river twice, the same technique and strategy will never be performed exactly the same way twice. The context of execution will always change.

Context is typically made up of three elements: task, performer, and environment. These elements are dynamic and interact with each other. The context of the game could include the length of the pass, the position of the ball, the position of teammates and opponents, the player's fatigue level, the player's confidence, elapsed time, the sun, the wind, and so on.

Taking a games-based approach during our practices helps us expose players to changing situations and conditions that simulate a real game. These situations aid the development of each player's technique and decision-making ability. We are developing their ability to perceive and recognize scenarios within the game along with their ability to take the correct action under the constraints context presents.

Playing games during practice creates learning that transfers to games. In this way, our players are given repeated exposure to game-like situations. They discover solutions and add skills to their toolkit. Their technique-and-strategy toolkit will be ready for their game.

Coach Eddie Jones, when serving as a rugby manager, offered an interesting perspective on this, stating that to create thinking players and ensure successful transfer of practice to competition, practice must be contextualized in conditions that replicate the game.[1] According to Coach Jones, games are complex and dynamic, and successful negotiation of the scenarios that confront players in games requires interaction with and simultaneous application of tactical awareness and knowledge, decision making, and skill execution.[2]

Our goal during practice is always twofold. One, provide a joyful experience to all participants; and two, create learning experiences that translate to the game. We want to develop skillful performers who play our games with passion and pride!

Best Practice Concepts

1. Create practice environments and activities that closely resemble a game and game conditions to teach both technique and strategy. Think practice activities, not drills.
2. Adjust and modify practice activities with age-appropriate rules, structures, and boundaries to better facilitate learning (i.e., exposure to the problem).
3. Organize players into small groups with limited or no wait time between practice activity or repetition. Lines should be no longer than three players: one practicing, one up next, one waiting. If your lines get longer than three, add another station, line, or goal.
4. Take advantage of the intrinsic motivation in children to play. Keep a high tempo and rhythm during practice. Practice flow should feel like a game.
5. Provide opportunities for players to score, succeed, and achieve during practice. Scoring or earning a goal or recognition encourages players to try again or reinforces a successful attempt. Environmental feedback is critical to learning and motivation for your players.
6. Use small-sided or modified game structures to increase repetition and interaction. Think increased opportunity to execute techniques and to engage strategic thinking and decision making.
7. Ensure that your coaching instruction and guidance connect the why, what, and how of executing technique and strategy.
8. Assume the role of facilitator. Be more a guide on the side rather than a sage on the stage.

9. Teach difficult skills or strategies. Draw analogies and use examples of activities from other sports to create connections. Use role models to demonstrate if needed.
10. Use video and video analysis when possible. For coaches of younger players, video feedback is for the coach's own use. As your teams transition to middle-school age, video can be shared as an additional instructional tool.

You have not taught until they've learned.—John Wooden

NOTES

1. Edwin Jones, "Transferring Skill from Practice to the Match in Rugby through Game Sense," *Active and Healthy Magazine* 22, nos. 2–3 (June 2015): 56–58.

2. P. Kinnerk, S. Harvey, C. MacDonncha, and M. Lyons, "A Review of the Game-Based Approaches to Coaching Literature in Competitive Team Sport Settings," *Quest* 70, no. 4 (2018): 401–18, doi:10.1080/00336297.2018.143939.

6

COACHING GAMES

There is something magical about games. Maybe it's the unknown. Perhaps it's the opportunity to potentially and positively influence the outcome. Involvement equals influence. Games are a performance stage, an opportunity to demonstrate skills and strategy. They give us a chance to compete fairly in a yet-to-be determined contest, a chance to shine under bright lights and scrutiny. Even if the game is being played by youngsters on a park field surrounded by parents in lawn chairs, it is the players' moment.

These moments bring joy: the joy of sharing a game with your teammates; the joy of testing yourself and your limits; the joy of discovering new and yet-unknown strengths; the joy of experiencing the thrill of victory or the agony of defeat. Games should provide a joyful moment of self-expression and experience for their players. Sometimes magic can be stressful. The magician makes a coin disappear for a moment, only to have it reappear behind your ear. Games have this magic too. Winning and losing create magical moments.

Games appear lost only to be rescued at the last moment for a victory. Games appear to be won only to be pulled away at the last moment for a loss. This uncertainty of result each time you play brings an important dose of stress to games. You can win. You can lose. And just like the coin trick, the thrill is in living the experience of playing the game.

Games are played by the players. It is imperative to recognize the person in the arena is the player, not the coaches, not the parents, not the fans, not management. Games belong to the players. The players are in the arena. Here is a statement on this from an authority.

> It is not the critic who counts; not the man who points out how the strong man stumbles, or where the doer of deeds could have done them better. The credit belongs to the man who is actually in the arena, who strives valiantly; who errs, who comes short again and again, because there is no effort without error; but who does actually strive to do the deeds; who knows great enthusiasms, the great devotions; who spends himself in a worthy cause; who knows the triumph of high achievement, and who at the worst, if he fails, at least fails while daring greatly, so that his place shall never be with those cold and timid souls who neither know victory nor defeat.—Theodore Roosevelt

THE BASIC GAME-DAY COACHING PROCESS AND PHILOSOPHY

As coaches we get to share in the beautiful experience of players playing the game. We join them on the sidelines, from the bench, and on pool decks. Surrounded by water bottles and snacks, we play an important role in their arena. We are privileged to share these moments.

We are responsible for creating a positive game experience and a performance platform for all our players. This includes preparing them to play during practice and coaching them during games. Coaching games is different from coaching practice. There are many unique components of games. Many of these are out of the direct control of the individual player: playing time, officials, opponents, outcomes. These external pressures and circumstances call on us as coaches to have a basic coaching process and philosophy.

This clear and simple philosophy can shine through the glare and pressure of games.

- acknowledge what is being done well by both team and player
- identify what can be improved or corrected
- plan for correcting and improving
- do what is needed

This process and philosophy permits you to identify what you control and what you influence. Appreciating this distinction allows coaching behavior and actions to be focused properly. This process and philosophy keeps the focus on the coaching role and lessens the need to try to play the game for the players.

Playing Time

Players want to play their game. Players need to play their game. It is our responsibility as coaches to find ways to maximize playing time for each player. Regardless of the age or level of the player, playing time is important. Players seek the opportunity to be in the game. Putting skills and strategies on display in front of a coach and against an opponent is empowering, thrilling, and rewarding.

For younger players the distinction between practice and games is smaller. The set-up and format are quite similar. There are fewer formalities for the coach to manage. However, as games get more structured, the perspective on playing time changes. Playing time is viewed as a finite resource. There is less to go around. How playing time is allotted while maximizing development becomes a challenge.

Maximizing playing time for each player runs counter to adult versions and viewpoints of games. Adults believe games should be played to win. In the adult world, outcomes demand performance, and the most-talented people should perform. The best players play. While this might be true in high-level, competitive environments and professional sports, this statement is too black-and-white for youth sports. Youth sports demand a different lens and more intricate perspective.

Our philosophies of and perspectives on playing time are often subconscious. We don't know how we truly feel about playing time and its role in a player's sport experience until we're faced with the final play in a game that's on the line. Who will we have in the game?

Games are an experiential learning environment. One must be completely involved in the game to reap all the benefits and experiences. Being involved means playing time. For each individual player this means starting games, finishing games, playing in big moments, playing in small moments, succeeding and failing.

Creating a healthy environment for playing time is paramount. A common cultural norm is that playing time is earned at practice. Giving clarity to this process of earning clarity is critical. With playing time as the lure, players are compliant at practice. They avoid mistakes and do as they are told. Playing time is earned. Non-compliance or mistakes result in decreased playing time, which is actively avoided.

The developmental level of your players is a key consideration for a healthy environment for playing time to exist. Players need opportunities to grow both during practice and in the games. This means playing time and freedom to experience the game. This is true regardless of the level of play. Playing in games matters.

Experiencing the game will result in both successes and mistakes. More-developed players at a higher competition level will make fewer mistakes during games. Appreciating these learning moments allows us to practice patience with our players. Players should be provided ample playing time to explore the game.

Players thrive in environments where playing time is an integral part of the learning process and not a separate universe for a select few. Under the bright lights of games, our coaching philosophies and beliefs are revealed.

Winners and Losers

Let's start this section with a simple question: How many of you out there would like to be a successful coach? We will assume that all of you have your hand raised. Here's another simple question, or perhaps not so simple: What is success?

Let's leave that up in the air awhile and do some exploring.

There are winners and there are losers. How can we separate the sheep from the goats?

Taking part in the 2019 New York Marathon were 30,794 men and 22,714 women. The first man to reach the finish line was Geoffrey Kamworor of Kenya at 2:08:13, nosing out Albert Korir, also of Kenya, at 2:08:36. Joyciline Jepkosgei of Kenya was the first woman finisher at 2.22:38, followed by Mary Keitany of Kenya at 2.23:32.

The television coverage focused on these four and numerous others who finished. There also was coverage of elderly persons, a heart-attack survivor, amputees, wheelchair contestants, and some first-timers. With that information, here are some questions for you to consider.

- Were Joyciline Jepkosgei and Geoffrey Kamworor the only winners and were the other 53,506 runners losers?
- Were the runners who met their goal of time or placement losers or were they winners?
- Were the many finishers who set a new personal record winners?
- Was Daniel Romanchuk of the United States, who led the men's wheelchair group, a winner?
- How about Marcel Hug of Switzerland, who came in .01 second behind him?
- The same questions can be asked about Manuela Schar of Switzerland and Tatyana McFadden of the United States, who came in first and second in the women's wheelchair group.
- And there are the same questions about the elderly and amputee participants.

Let's take a broader view. Who determines whether you are a winner or a loser? Can you decide if someone else is a winner or a loser? How often do we allow others to judge whether we are successful and how much judging of others do we do? And then the biggest question after you decide who the losers are: What do you do with them?

WINNERS IN THE SURVIVAL GAME

Business leaders, the smart ones, know that survival of the fittest isn't productive if taken to an extreme. There can be only one CEO, but you can't kill off the rest of the organization. Everyone in the corporation must believe that he or she is a winner: the comptroller, the sales manager, the plant manager, the foreman on the line, the die maker, the typist, the janitor. If you make any of them losers, you diminish the whole company.

There is an important distinction to be made here between finite and infinite games. A finite game has a clear ending, and there is competition to win the game. The competitors in a finite game try to be first and in front. An infinite game involves a different approach. An infinite game is ongoing. The competitors in an infinite game recognize that sometimes they'll be first and ahead and sometimes they won't. The goal is to keep growing and processing. Video games are formatted this way: fail, learn, grow, respawn, and play again, always progressing.

Understanding the game you're playing is key. Viewing games as either finite or infinite has a profound impact on how players are defined. Losing a game does not make you a loser. What you do and who you are are two different things. You can lose and not be a loser. You can be, act, and feel like a winner regardless of the circumstances. And so it is with a team. The players, the batboys, the parents, the assistant coaches, and you must all feel that you are winners. You might want to consider the effect of making some of your players winners and the others losers. If any of your players feel inadequate, the whole team suffers.

QUALITIES OF A WINNER

Are we focused too much on winning? Do you have to win the World Series, the Super Bowl, the Indy 500, Wimbledon, or any other sports equivalent in order to be a winner? We hope not! Because if being a winner demands that level of achievement, most of us are losers.

Even winners aren't always a winner. Even the greatest athletes lose now and then. At the same time, though, they aren't losers. They're always working toward excellence in performance and toward fulfilling their potential as athletes.

Take, for example, Ernie Banks and Billy Williams of the Chicago Cubs, both excellent players, both members of the Baseball Hall of Fame, who were denied the honor of being on a pennant-winning team and appearing in the World Series. They showed up for every game and always gave their best.

We could go on and name many of the greatest athletes in sports history who didn't reach an ultimate goal. Sam Snead never won the U.S. Open; Pete Sampras never won the French Open; Jim Ryun, the greatest miler of his time, was knocked down in a qualifying heat and didn't win the 1,500-meter run in the Olympics; Glen Cunningham was frustrated in his pursuit of the four-minute mile; and who can forget Mary Decker falling in the finals at the 1984 Olympics?

Were any of these great athletes losers? Of course not. They pursued excellence, they worked diligently to fulfill their potential as athletes, and they gave us a glimpse of what the human quest is.

THE QUALITIES OF GREAT ATHLETES

Let's examine the qualities that great athletes exhibit in their pursuit of excellence so that we can get some insight on how we should deal with our own players. Here is a short list.

Pride: Your players must be proud of themselves, proud of their team, proud of their own actions and achievements, proud of their coach.

Discipline: Discipline is the setting of goals and then moving toward them with a sense of purpose and responsibility.

Self-reliance: The one critical responsibility we have to our players is to make them self-reliant, to work with them so that they become independent of us.

Dedication and Hard Work: These are the sweat-related qualities your players need to develop in order to make everything work.

We need to give our players roots and wings—it doesn't work unless they have both.

EXCELLENCE CREATES EXCELLENCE

A good friend told us this story.

> I was coaching basketball at a small high school in central Illinois. We had a very good team, and even though we had only one hundred students we played anybody and always had at least a 75 percent winning record. However, when the state tournament began, we had to go through county playoffs against other small schools and some of these teams tended to be poor to awful in quality.
>
> I recall one game when our kids started out running our offense beautifully. Our fast break was going well, our offense was smooth—we looked great. The other team, however, seemed to know very little about defense, and every time one of our players should have been clear, driving around a screen and going in for a lay-up, one of

the opponents who had lost his man was standing around clogging up the player's lane. Likewise, there didn't seem to be any pattern or structure to their offense.

Before long, my team lost its sparkle and excellence—our terrific fast break was slowed to a walk, and we reverted to "alley basketball." We won the game, but that night we were not the team that had stood up against the best teams in the state. We played only a bit better than our opponents. Fortunately, as the tournament went on we met better teams and we managed to regain our excellence.

The point of this story is that our challengers are much more than our opponents—they are the co-creators of an environment that enables us, that forces us, to express our excellence. We must honor those players, those teams that challenge us. It is because of their excellence that we play so well. Make sure you give those folks you really want to beat, and beat soundly, the credit they deserve for being there and taking you on.

HONORING THE GAME

The game is a sacred space. It has a life force all its own. This space and all those who enter it deserve the utmost respect. There is an inherent privilege in playing the game. This privilege includes the responsibility of playing the game the right way. Our actions and beliefs must reflect the sanctity of the game.

Our opponents matter. We are in fact collaborators in a positive and high-performance environment. Together we co-create a competitive environment. This relationship deserves recognition and acknowledgement.

Referees and officials are an essential part of the game. They share in the privilege of participation in and responsibility for this co-creation. They are protecting fair and spirited competition while ensuring the safety of the players. Their job requires a knowledge of rules and strategies and the ability to supervise and keep under control all aspects of the game. Officials deserve our respect and honor as they execute this role to the best of their ability.

It is important to recognize that an official might never have scored a basket, blocked a puck, or aced a serve. These actions belong to the athletes. Frustration with execution sometimes needs a convenient outlet. Officials often bear the brunt of our feelings and become the frustration focal point for players and coaches. Demonstrating clear respect for officials and their integrity goes a long way toward honoring the game. Are you the kind of coach or athlete who needs your opponent to fail for you to win? Or are you good enough to beat the other team when they are playing their best?

SPORTSMANSHIP: HOW WE COMPETE AND PLAY

Here's a thought from Cindy Bristow when she was serving with USA Softball. "In any type of athletic contest, a true champion wants their opponent to play their very best; then they know they are truly champions. You are encouraging others to be successful and, in effect, celebrating their success."

Reality is often quite different. At a typical game, unfortunately, you will likely experience players, coaches, fans clapping, cheering, and mocking mistakes and errors made by the opposite side. As far as they're concerned, winning is all that counts even if it is through the failure of others rather than the product of high-level performance.

A powerful message is being sent to and interpreted by your players: fear of failure. Players can feel this in a game. Fear of failure means that your players will shy away from experimenting with new skills, trying new tactics, or creating new ideas.

Learning is the companion of mistakes. Young players are still growing and discovering their coordination and athleticism. Errors common in the beginning will be accompanied by gradual improvement over time. Even as adults we are learning. We fail, we learn, and we grow. What's the primary difference between ourselves and our young players? We usually don't have others clapping for or jeering at our errors or mistakes. Can you imagine everyone in the copy room clapping as you struggle over the copy machine or a sarcastic slow clap from across the conference-room table when you misspeak during a presentation?

We need to teach our players the next level of sportsmanship: competing fairly and in earnest with a real respect for the game and our opponents. Role-modeling good sportsmanship means providing space and grace for your players to make mistakes. They need our support and smiles—not jeers and rolled eyes with words mumbled under our breath.

Trial and error lead to a process of on-going self-discovery. Mistakes are a key to growing. No player deliberately strikes out, throws a gutter ball, forgets to touch the wall on the turn, touches the ball before the putt. We need to provide an environment and role-model behavior that promotes sportsmanship.

COACHING GAMES

Game day is a magical time. Practice is behind us. Preparation has planted the seeds of confidence. Pre-game nerves are communicating with us, telling us that we want to do well. Cleaned and pressed jerseys are ready. We have the privilege of putting on a uniform and performing in the arena.

A real privilege of coaching happens on game day, the privilege of leading our players as they enter the arena. This is a treasured responsibility. Our responsibility goes far beyond our clipboard with game plans and special plays. Our approach, as a coach, to game day sets the tone for our entire pack. The behavior we role-model is the behavior we'll likely witness in return. What kind of game experience do we want to create for our players?

Throwing fits and ranting on the sidelines during the game will be returned in kind by our players and their parents. Shouting instructions and joy-sticking every player action will result in uniformed robots and not creative, thoughtful players. Subconscious and unwanted emotions can surface under the pressure of game day.

Remembering that coaches don't score touchdowns, win races, hit homeruns, or make game-saving plays should relieve some of the pressure. Our game-day role is serving the players and honoring the game. Our actions and behavior should guide our players to the performance of a lifetime or just the best they can do on a brisk Saturday afternoon.

Truly observing the game is paramount. What's actually happening? The emotions of the game must be properly managed. Our coaching focus and efforts need to be on finding moments to guide and mentor our players. This means allowing the game to unfold and the players to play. Trying to coach and instruct in the heat of the moment means you're already coaching in the past. The game unfolds faster than our minds can process and our voices shout.

Allow your players to experience their game. Permit players to truly live in the arena. Protecting this sacred space for your players will increase your instructional opportunities. By giving the players room to do their very best we create space for ourselves to coach. If doing their best isn't good enough for us and for that crowd in the stands then we're having these kids play the game for the wrong reasons.

Grace's Advice

I recall a moment in my basketball coaching career. I had been doing a lot of yelling at the players from the bench, and my older sister, Grace, who was quite a fan, asked me why I did that. My team's win-loss record was good and my kids were playing their very best. As younger brothers do, I didn't think much of her comment, but early in the next game I discovered myself giving a lot of advice to my players in a loud voice from the bench, and I stopped. I sat back and watched the game.

And do you know that my kids kept on playing good basketball and we kept our record up? I suspect that they liked the change. For one thing, they stopped looking at the bench so much and concentrated on the game better. And finally, I found myself enjoying the game more.

Postgame

Time has expired. The clock is at zero. The race is complete. Now what? Our post-game responsibilities are critical. Every player needs to depart a champion.

In any type of athletics, a true champion wants his or her opponent to play their very best because then they know they truly are a champion! Signs of appreciation and sportsmanship should be proudly displayed at the end of every game. High fives, handshakes, and fist bumps should be freely given to opponents and officials alike. Role-modeling this behavior sends a clear message to everyone on how to honor the game even after the final whistle.

Your players are covered with mud and dirt. There are visible grass stains on jerseys and socks and invisible feelings about a just-completed individual performance. Victorious or defeated, our players look to us to help them successfully transition out of the arena with our post-game talk.

You know that emotions are high for both you and the players. This is not the time for long-winded speeches as parents sit impatiently in their cars. Post-game talks need to get to the point. Bring the team together for a bit of processing and perspective. They just competed and collaborated in a game that is now behind them. Moving players forward requires taking a quick look in the rearview mirror.

First, check in quickly and make sure everyone is healthy and okay. Then share with them what they did well. Have each player visualize a few successful plays they made. Point out how good this feels. Then allow the players to share their thoughts and feelings about the game, but only in positive terms. No excuses. No complaining. No alibis or blaming someone else. Any negative statements should be followed immediately by "Delete, Delete." Players catch on to this process very quickly and jump right in.

If there are any awards, this is a good time to hand them out. If any goals have been reached, comment on them. Note the next practice or game scheduled. Clearly express your appreciation and gratitude for their efforts in the game they just played. If they have played a terrible game, this is your opportunity to show some real class. Show the same appreciation as if they had played their best. This is one of the marks of the inspirational coach.

Regardless of the outcome, send your team toward their post-game ice-cream cone with a renewed spirit and determination to grow.

The Next Practice

The next practice provides an ideal opportunity to constructively debrief the most recent game. Everyone has had time for processing and reflection. Modeling this reflection process and dialogue is critical to both individual growth and team improvement.

This is not the time to give personal affirmations—the time for that has passed. This is a meeting of the team (the pack). This is not the time to chastise a player in front of his or her teammates. There is never a time for that. This is the time to deal with the reason we play the game. We are better people and better players for having played the game.

There are three issues that you need to explore.

- What went well during the game?
- What still needs work?
- Why are we better for having played that game?

These three issues are inherently connected and interrelated. That is why they have not been numbered. As you talk about what went well, you may hear someone say, "But we could have been even better if . . ." and the path to improvement has taken the floor.

A Peek Inside the Next Practice

Head Coach: "Okay, what went well in the game on Saturday?"

Player: "I liked how we kept covering up for each other when someone got into trouble."

Player: "Yeah, I liked doing that. We cut out their easy back-door baskets."

Coach: "I liked how you all went after loose balls. That shows real desire. We also let them score too easily when they intercepted that pass. We will work on that today."

Player: "I had trouble getting the ball inbounds at the end of the game."

Coach: "That's a good point. We need to show you how to get open for the inbound pass better."

Player: "We lost but I thought we did a lot better talking to each other."

Coach: "How do some of the rest of you feel about that?"

Several Players: "Yeah, that was good." [A lot of nodding heads.]

Coach: "What about that big argument you got into with the official?"

Player: "I gave the ref a look, a mean one, but no one got into trouble."

Coach: "Exactly. I want to compliment you all for keeping your cool. You handled it well. No technical. You showed real class."

Coach: "Last week we set a goal to make fewer sloppy fouls. How did we do with that goal?"

Assistant Coach: "There were only two sloppy fouls." [Everyone laughs.]

Coach: "I want you to let go of everything you didn't do as well as you wanted and hang on to what you learned from that game. I think we're ready to have a good practice."

On to the next one.

7

PARTNERING WITH PARENTS

Who are the members of the pack? The kids, the parents of the kids, and the coaches. This relationship takes us to another element: the parents of our players. What is their role? Basically, it is to be totally supportive of their child and the coach. There's more to this, and we'll be telling you about things such as knowing the rules of the game and so forth, let's first agree that we're going to work together on this project so the kids will have a great experience.

It is important that the parents understand that they are members of the pack along with their child and the coaches. Let's deal with this responsibility in the most positive manner that is available to us. There are three elements: the coaches, the kids, and the parents of these kids.

How do coaches and1 parents work together so that their kids have the best experience possible? It is essential that all the individuals involved communicate openly and clearly with one another. They shouldn't fall into the trap of hiding their discoveries or ideas so that they can one-up their associates. If they do, the whole project is in jeopardy. Kids, parents, and the coach are *all* members of the pack.

Being a member of the pack for parents simply means joining up with their kids and the coaches so that their kids have a joyful, productive, successful life experience.

We have all heard of or seen instances of parents being out of control at sports events (yelling at officials, at opposing team members, at their own coach, and even at their own kids) or of parents making impossible demands (Why isn't my Jimmy the quarterback?). The basic

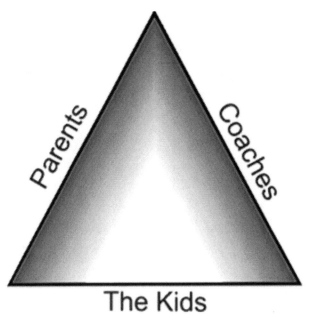

Partners with kids. *Courtesy of Peter S. Pierro.*

problem underlying this kind of behavior is parents mistaking their role and responsibilities relative to the activity.

Mr. Joe Smith is not going to be standing on the free throw line in the last second of the game with a chance to first tie and then win the basketball game. Mrs. Clara Jones is not going to be standing at the top of the slalom course as the start buzzer beeps. Their children are in the arena. It is their game.

Joe and Clara are spectators and support people. Those are their correct roles, and they must learn how to be responsible, caring experts in those roles. The kids are the people who really count. The rest of the staging and the adults are there to make this work out right for the kids so let's make sure that whatever we add to the activity enhances it, makes it better for them.

WE HAVE THE SAME GOALS!

It's clear that as we communicate with one another we must come to realize that we, the coaches, and the parents are on the same side. We want the same things. We have common goals in this venture, and we have to focus on these goals and not allow selfish, egocentric goals to get in the way. The focus throughout this book has been the basic fact that this game is for the kids. We adults come along on this venture to make sure that it is a great experience for them.

What are our common goals? All of them involve the different aspects of sportsmanship.

1. Our kids will have a great time.
2. Our kids will learn new skills.
3. Our kids will improve their physical abilities.
4. Our kids will learn about this great game, its rules, its history, its place in the world.
5. Our kids will form new, worthwhile relationships with fellow team players.
6. Our kids will compete responsibly with the players on opposing teams.
7. Our kids will learn new, positive forms of personal responsibility and self-discipline.
8. Our kids will learn to deal positively with authority figures; for example, coaches and officials.
9. Our kids will have great respect for the game, for their coaches, for their parents, for the officials, and above all, for themselves.
10. Our kids will become well-rounded individuals with great personal growth and a sense of who they are and how they relate to and interact with the people in their lives.

That is our list of common goals. You may want to add to or subtract from this list. You and the parents may want to personalize it and rewrite it in this way:

Jeanne will have a great time.
Jeanne will learn new skills.
Jeanne will . . .

Put these goals in your team newsletter and insist that all the players' parents subscribe to them and treat their kids accordingly. Insist that all the coaches subscribe to them and coach the kids accordingly. Insist that your league officials subscribe to them and run the league accordingly.

When do parents allow their children to become adults? Many parents accompany their children to tryouts and practices and try to have some influence on how their offspring are treated: what position they play, where they are in the batting order, if they are in the starting line-up, and so on. Old habits are hard to break, and some parents may have been doing this since their kids were six years old or even younger. They may not have a clear idea of whether their children are able, and required, to make their own decisions. If you're not an Olympic-level coach or if you're coaching at the college level or below, you must work with parents, and the younger the player the more intense the criticism, the questions, and the advice. You can make that a problem or you can make it an opportunity.

LEADERSHIP MODELS TO USE WITH PARENTS

There are two opposite ways to deal with the parents of your players. The first is an autocratic position. The autocratic coach has no interaction with the parents. She is the coach and she makes all the decisions with no outside interference. This will work as long as she never loses a game.

The second position is a blend of authoritative and transformational leadership. This coach chooses to bring the parents in as part of the whole team process. We will be taking and promoting this position for the rest of this section.

Briefly put, you either accept parents as partners or you keep them totally out of the picture. Any middle position will get you into trouble. You need an overall philosophy of working with parents in the partnership mode. This philosophy will help you guide, mentor, educate, and include the parents as members of the pack.

Here are some ideas that you can share with parents on becoming expert support persons and worthwhile members of the pack.

- Learn the rules of the game or activity so that your comments are helpful. For example, it's not a good idea to yell at the umpire when he makes the correct call on a pop-up and you don't know the infield fly rule.
- Learn the strategies of the game so you don't yell at your child to stay on their man in a basketball game when the team is playing a zone defense. It's also good to know the three-second lane rule.
- Learn the skills and tactics of the activity so that you can be a positive support to the coach. Don't ever say "Coach told you to grip the club that way but she's wrong; the overlap grip is the only right one." Never force your child to make a choice between what the coach tells her to do and what you tell her to do.
- Know the correct behavior and involvement as a fan and parent. Cheer "Hit it" like crazy when your child is batting in a softball game and don't yell "Miss it" when your child's opponent is shooting a free throw.
- Know your child's skills, his readiness to use them, and his emotional and psychological status in dealing with them. Is he ready to hit a curveball? Can he deal with losing a game? Winning a game? Can he deal with sitting on the bench?
- Learn all you can about coaching. Don't get on the coach's back on every issue that arises and every decision he makes. However, it is your responsibility to learn what the coach can and should be doing with your child.
- Keep in mind that your child's team is a peer group and that it can have a very strong, positive effect. Almost all the peer groups we join in schools, churches, sports activities, and so on foster positive, growth-creating experiences.
- Above all, be a champion for your child. Protect her from physical and psychological abuse (including your own).

Remember, parents help their children through many of life's major developmental milestones. Parents patiently wait for their children's muscles and for their sense of balance, desire, and confidence to sufficiently develop to accomplish the task of walking.

Parents' love for their children should not depend on whether they win or lose in a kids' game or whether they get the lead in a school play or help move the scenery onstage. Coaches can provide helpful reminders to parents that their love for their children should be constant regardless of the results of any activity.

As partners, parents and coaches share in the responsibility of co-creating a healthy, joyful, and productive experience for every child who participates. Coaches and parents must model positive and proper behavior and sportsmanship. The kids are the essential characters in playing the game or engaging in the activity.

Mentoring Matters

In partnering with the parents of your players, you as the coach must understand that mentoring matters. Being familiar with the important topics below will help you provide substantive mentorship and guidance to parents.

Growth, Development, and Maturation

In previous chapters, we dealt with concepts such as growth, development, and maturation. Now we have to look at what these concepts mean when we are working with the parents of our kids. Growth and development are fairly simple. You and Mr. and Mrs. Gibson know that Chris has grown two inches and gained fifteen pounds since last season. These qualities are measurable and concrete. We also know that Chris's cognitive growth has changed but we don't know how to measure that change. These changes and concepts come under the heading of maturation.

Maturation has to be seen as many different factors and states. These states and factors include competition, teamwork, winning, losing, skills development, strategies of the game, responsibility to other people, and representation of other groups.

Rather than giving you a definition, we want to pose some questions having to do with maturation. These questions are not in any chronological order. Take time with each of these and imagine you're dealing with a concerned parent of Chris (who may be either male or female).

- At what age does Chris realize that she is competing with someone else?

- At what age does Chris realize that he is supposed to cooperate with someone else? When is he supposed to work well with others?
- At what age is Chris aware that she is a member of a group called a team and she must include them in her play? What is her responsibility in this?
- At what age is Chris aware that he is representing an organization called a school and that his school is competing with a different school? What is his responsibility in this venture?
- At what age does Chris realize that winning is something and that losing is something?
- At what age does Chris understand that winning is good and losing is bad?
- At what age does Chris understand the concept of sportsmanship?
- At what age can Chris learn the skills needed to play the game? Is that the same age at which he must learn the strategies of the game?
- At what age can Chris deal with rules? Does she understand what penalties are?

Handling a Problem with Parents

Coaches are continually confronted with problems that require them to deal with the parents of their players. Usually the involved parent and the coach see the player from a different point of view. There are many stories and even movies based on this problem. We see something from our point of view while dealing with people who see it from their point of view. We call this "selective perception." Selective perception is a perceptual process in which a person perceives only what he desires to and sets aside or ignores other perceptions or viewpoints.

A Coach-Parent Scenario

Let me introduce you to Lucy and have you become her coach for a while. Lucy is Mrs. Stone's daughter but on the ballfield she is your player. You and Mrs. Stone are watching Lucy field grounders. She is concerned about Lucy's ability but she can see some improvement in her playing. She hopes that Lucy will get a starting position—probably as shortstop.

In the meantime, you are comparing Lucy to Latisha and finding Lucy behind her in ability and maturity. You plan to select Latisha for the position.

Let's clarify this situation.

Mrs. Stone is watching her daughter Lucy and she sees her performing better than Latisha or anyone else for the position. You are watching a player trying out for an infield position and comparing her performance to that of other players—especially Latisha's. You and Mrs. Stone are not seeing the same thing. You can, and must, be objective and realistic in your decision. Though objectivity might be possible when another parent looks at their own child, Mrs. Stone isn't objective—this is her daughter we're dealing with.

Recently Mrs. Stone has been letting you know that she thinks Lucy is the best choice for shortstop. You listen to Mrs. Stone's thoughts and feelings and determine if they have validity and should be added to your information in making your decision. Latisha's parents have not been heard from on this issue.

What are you going to do in this situation?

If you are a disengaged (laissez-faire) coach, you don't even know this is a situation. As far as you're concerned, out of sight is out of mind and whatever will be will be. Everything will work out fine. (We will not suggest that this is a way to deal with any kind of coaching situation.) If you are a command coach, you make the decision and you don't care what anybody else thinks about it. You don't want to know, or care to know, what Mrs. Stone thinks.

However, you are a transformer coach. You have to acknowledge that Mrs. Stone has a point of view and that your point of view is different from hers. You also know that it is your responsibility to the team to make the best decisions for the team. You are also invested in the belief that parents are members of the team. You also accept that this is an important situation that must be given consideration so as to prevent its having a negative effect on the team.

There is the possibility that this issue will cause a breakdown in the coach-parent partnership. What should you do?

You do what is best for the team: you choose the better player.

THE PERSON, THE PLAYER, THE PERFORMER

The three *P*s are very well known among coaches, and unlike many sayings it makes a lot of sense when it is used appropriately and caringly. Remember, this is an important principle of coaching. We coach the person first. We treat the person entirely as a person—a living, growing, developing human being. Competition enters this person's life in everyday incidents and simple games with siblings, classmates, and friends.

The person will become a player in real-life situations by playing games as part of their social life. They then may become a performer as they represent some entity such as their junior high basketball team.

Where Does This Go? Healthy Competition

Healthy competition can be good for kids. Competitive activities help develop important skills for life. They create foundations and habits for how to handle wins and losses later in life.

Our games and competitive activities teach both character and life traits. This begins with learning how to cooperate, share, and take turns. And this can evolve into a growth mindset, resiliency, and empathy. There are endless possible lessons within sports if we're willing to look beyond the concept of winning and losing.

Healthy competition allows us to embrace all the aspects of sports. Find and celebrate the lessons that are just under the surface. A persistent myth is that winning is everything. This myth has shaped the view of countless coaches and parents. Moving beyond this myth calls for acknowledging other more important lessons.

Children involved in healthy competition could be:

- ask to play again (with tremendous enthusiasm!)
- handle winning and losing with grace and perspective
- discover internal motivation
- experience improved self-esteem

Children involved in unhealthy competition may:

- actively resist participating

- find ways not to participate, including forgetting equipment or faking illness
- say they want to quit

Healthy competition can become a garden where character traits bloom for children. We as coaches get to cultivate this learning garden and help our parents understand the inherent beauty in this opportunity. This is the person-player-performer culture.

Promoting the character trait–building component of sport is next-level coaching. It keeps the focus in the right place: on the person. Games with healthy competition benefit the entire person. These games encourage the social, emotional, physical, and even spiritual growth of our players. We have the privilege to move our coaching beyond winning trophies toward a brighter horizon.

Legendary coach John Wooden recognized this synergy and connection between winning and cultivating character. And what was the highest level of success for Coach Wooden? He stated, "Success is a peace of mind which is a direct result of self-satisfaction in knowing that you did your best to become the best you are capable of becoming."

It is a journey and process to become the best version of yourself. Developing and growing your unlimited capability is not just about talent. Talent alone is never enough to reach your full potential. Character counts. Competition creates a platform where we cultivate character. Like a teeter-totter, this platform is mobile. It provides an opportunity to develop and display positive and healthy character traits or to surface negative and unhealthy traits. Participants (players, coaches, officials, parents, fans, etc.) in sports are given an opportunity to act in and react to various and fast-changing scenarios.

Becoming a person of character calls for a commitment to a standard of action. Responding appropriately to life's challenges and successes takes practice and patience. Guidance and insight are required from coaches and parents. Helping others develop their personal code of conduct is another one of a coach's gifts and responsibilities.

All of us are unique, and we should all be treated as unique people. In the dealings we have described above, there are differences among all of the players. This is the joy and pain of every parent, teacher, and coach—that is, those of us who deal with these unique people. You may even run into a late-developing child so maybe, just maybe, you need to have patience.

The George Mikan Story

If a game-show host ever asks you who the outstanding basketball player of the first half of the twentieth century was and you want to be a millionaire, you must choose George Mikan. His story is an inspiration for all clumsy kids.

Mikan played with the Minneapolis Lakers in the late 1940s and early 1950s. He was 6 feet, 10 inches tall, a standout giant in those days. As a high school student in Joliet, Illinois, and as a freshman at Notre Dame, he had been an unsuccessful, overgrown, clumsy youth. In 1943, he enrolled at DePaul University in Chicago under Coach Ray Meyer. Coach Meyer saw an awkward giant trying to play basketball. However, he saw something else: a young man with dreams and the determination to work toward them. The Coach, as he became known, spent hours on end working with Mikan, and the results are in.

Mikan was an All American in 1944, 1945, and 1946. He led DePaul to the championship of the biggest college tournament of that time, the National Invitational Tournament, in 1945. He then led the Lakers to six titles in the NBA; was individual scoring leader for three years; was on the All-Star team every year that he played; was elected to the Naismith Memorial Hall of Fame; and to cap it off, in a special poll taken in 1950, was named the greatest basketball player in the first half of the twentieth century.

That's what a little dedication and hard work can do for you, and it tells us a lot about Ray Meyer and why he was such a successful coach. What if he had cut Mikan from his Blue Demon squad? Would Mikan have gone to another school or would that have been the last in a series of failure messages, the straw that broke the camel's back? I wonder if he ever thought about giving up on himself.

You may want to read about another basketball player, one voted the best basketball player of the second half of the twentieth century—a fellow by the name of Michael Jordan—and find out how he got along in his high school career.

WHERE HAVE ALL THE THREE-SPORT LETTER-WINNERS GONE?

University of Oklahoma fans are proud of their former quarterback and Heisman Trophy winner Sam Bradford. He became an NFL quarterback with the St. Louis Rams and was named Rookie Offensive Player of the Year in 2010. His physical and leadership abilities always demonstrated the potential that this young man had.

There is another side of Sam that is probably even more important for parents and coaches to explore. From newspaper articles, we find that he was a three-letter man at Putnam City North High School, playing football, basketball, and golf. He also played hockey at a high level. It is more common for athletes coming from a large high school such as Putnam City North to specialize in one sport, such as football. In their early years they play football in season, attend football sports camp, play it informally with their teammates—just kind of being a football player all year long.

There is so much carryover from one sport to another that is valuable in terms of skills, attitudes, teamwork, and game strategies. For another reason, spending all year on one sport can get really exhausting (even boring). Why not swim or play volleyball or hockey in that off-season period?

Coaches and parents, give your athlete child a chance to explore as many sports as possible. Otherwise you may never know where his or her greatest abilities and interests are.

PLAYERS AND SELF-ESTEEM

An extremely important job that we have as coaches and parents is to help our players develop a good self-concept, a solid foundation that they can build the rest of their lives on. Self-esteem is a deep, usually hidden feeling that we have about ourselves, about whether we are okay or not okay. Even though we aren't too clear about this feeling, it controls most of what we do, what we think, and how we feel.

There must be an expectation that the sports activities that our players engage in will result in them having a more positive self-esteem. This is the responsibility of the coaches and parents, and it can be done.

Let's tune in on some of our players as they talk about their coaches and self-esteem.

Goal Number 1: Self-Identity

Hi! My name is Dotty. One of the things I like about my coach is that he always makes me feel that I am important. He calls me by my name, none of this "Hey, you" or "Hey, kid." One of the first things he did in spring practice was to sit down with each of us and get to know something about us as individuals. He also wanted to know what I expected to get out of playing with this team, what position I wanted to play, who my sports heroes are, and a lot of other stuff.

He never embarrasses any of us. He just expects us to do our best, and he lets us know when we don't live up to it. I know he likes me. He likes every one of us and he lets us know it. I guess what I like most of all about him is that he really believes in me.

Goal Number 2: Belonging and Community

Hi! My name is Gus. My coach is always talking about the pack. It would drive us crazy except that he really believes that stuff and he makes us believe it. I'll never forget the first day of practice. He handed out the uniforms and had us go into the restroom and put them on. Then he had a photographer take our pictures alone and with the whole team. At the next practice, he gave us a copy of our own picture and a team picture. He told us to put the team picture and our own picture up where we can see them every day. He said to remember that we are always individuals but that we also are members of this team. We should all know that we belong to this team and that the team belongs to us. I really like knowing that there's a bunch of people around who care about me and want me to be in their group.

Goal Number 3: Power and Input

Hi! My name is Gina. I guess I've always been kind of strong headed. I just want to know that people are listening to me. Sometimes I just dig my heels in the ground and refuse to listen or do anything. Coach does things a little different. For example, she holds these meetings at practice and lets us tell her what some of our ideas are. She never says "That's a stupid idea" or uses any other put-downs. She really listens, and I know she thinks about how good our ideas are. I don't know how, but Coach seemed to know right off the bat how I feel about things. She called me aside the other day and said, "Gina, I've been watching you and I think that you could become a good leader. I'm going to be asking you to help me with some of my work as the season goes along. What do you think?" I told her okay, and like the other day when we got a new player, she had me introduce her around and show her the ropes. I think we're going to get along okay.

Goal Number 4: Success Experiences

Hi! My name is Al. My coach is a bug on setting goals. He asked us to write down what we wanted to accomplish this summer with the team. I said I wanted to play in every game, be on the championship team, and go to the tournament.

He thought that was all right but asked me to go on from there, to say what I would have to do in order to get there. Well, I thought that I could improve my pass receiving, shooting, and passing accuracy. I'm sure keeping the other guys on the team on their toes when I'm passing.

So what is happening? I'm doing better on all three of them. But what I'm getting at is that I'm reaching goals that I set for myself and that those are the important goals. Winning is great but there are other things that are important too. Oh, Coach had us all agree on a team goal that we would be good sportsmen, and it's working. I guess the best thing that I could say is that I'm having fun this year.

Goal Number 5: Knowledge of Growth

Hi! I'm Tony and I think my coach is the greatest. What I like best is our after-game meetings. Coach calls them her debriefing sessions, whatever that means. Anyway, we sit down, and she goes over the things that we didn't do so good and she says to "let 'em go" and not to take them home with us—that we'll work on them next practice. And then she tells us to remember the things that we did right and to hang on to them.

I like how she tells us what we did right and what we did wrong. She's never "How many times have I told you to pass a goal kick wide?" Instead she says, "Remind me to have you work on your goal kicks." She doesn't beat you over the head with what you did wrong, she works on getting you to do it right. I always know what Coach is thinking about my game because she tells me. My coach last year used to yell at us a lot. She just told us what we were doing wrong, sometimes she just yelled at us. We didn't even know what she was yelling about. I didn't like that.

COMMUNICATING WITH PARENTS

Team Meetings

Sending a weekly or biweekly email message is a good idea. Ask one of your parents to do this. Give out general news—nothing personal. You may get personal with little notes to parents: "Glen has been working hard on his bunting in practice and in the last game his sacrifice bunt made it possible for us to tie the score and later win" or "I was really impressed with Lana last game. Even though the game looked lost, she kept encouraging everybody and we kept playing our best. We didn't win the game but Lana showed us how to be a winner."

In addition to your preseason and postseason meetings, you may need to call a special meeting to deal with a specific problem. Stay focused and keep your player's parents focused on that issue.

Danger! Danger! Don't get into the middle of a conflict between Alice's mom and dad—that is their problem to deal with. Stay away from the disagreement between the Nelsons and the Jacksons. Conflict between families will inevitably bleed out to include and impact the players, making it a team issue.

The Team-Parent Agreement

Below you'll find an agreement that can be made between parents and coaches having to do with the parents' commitment to their child and player. It must be dealt with cooperatively by the parents and the coaches. Any disagreements may be stated at the bottom of the form under Comments/Disclaimers. Parents may refuse to sign the form, but it must be returned. The coaches and parents will then have to get together and decide if the player should be allowed to play under those conditions.

The Team/Parent Agreement

As a parent of _____, I am also a member of the _____ team. I must and will work together with the coaches, game officials, and league officials to make this as good an experience as possible for _____. In order to do this, I must be as concerned about my behavior as I am about the behavior of our players.

I understand that _____ is the one and only person whose goals and aspirations count in this venture. My personal goals and aspirations should be met in other ways.

I understand that along with the coaches and the players I am a role model for the behavior of _____, the other players, the coaches, the parents of the other players, and any spectators.

I understand that _____ can respond to only one coach at a time—that my child cannot deal with advice from more than one source at a time. I also understand that what I perceive and what the coach perceives may be different and in conflict.

I understand that the best environment for my child to grow personally must have a minimum of stress, conflict, and disagreement.

I understand that one of the most important lessons that my child can learn is the value of sportsmanship and good manners.

I understand that one of the major goals of sports is for each participant to respect all other participants including teammates, opponents, coaches, officials, and parents.

Therefore, I will:

1. Support my child totally in this venture.
2. Support the coaches in their work to make this experience a good one for my child.
3. Support the game officials and other league officials in their work.
4. Assist the coaches and officials in keeping the game as sportsman-like and enjoyable for the players as possible.

5. Act as a positive role model for my child and for the other players, parents, and spectators.

I will not:

1. Use my child to fulfill my personal goals.
2. Use abusive or offensive language toward anyone.
3. Yell at the officials—it's the coach's job to argue responsibly.
4. Make my child or anyone else feel guilty or bad in any way for any reason.
5. Get on my child for honest errors and mistakes. He or she is learning how to play.

Signature _____

Comments/Disclaimers:

_____

8

MOVING FORWARD

The Best Is Yet to Come!

Throughout this book, we have shared many perspectives, insights, and beliefs about coaching. We have examined leading yourself as a coach, leading teams and players, coaching games, and partnering with parents. Adding practical knowledge and applicable skills to your coaching toolbox has been our goal. As you prepare to move forward on your coaching journey, we present one additional lens through which to view sports: competition.

THE LEVELS OF COMPETITION: A TAXONOMICAL TREATMENT

Competition, the quality that includes winning and losing, exists in many forms and levels throughout our lives. It grows and becomes more complex at succeeding stages. Relative to this context, we can express competition in a taxonomical format, from simple to complex.

We have adopted *the person*, *the player*, and *the performer* as the identities of the individual in this format. At each stage or level, we can describe the identity of the individual involved as acting in one or more of these roles. Defining these roles and identities helps us as coaches to understand and clarify the relationship individuals have with sports competition.

For example, for the very young child, games such as hide-and-seek are played with no indicators of winning or winner or losing or loser being expressed. The concept of winning and losing will change and evolve as the child becomes increasingly involved with sports as a player and as a performer. This type of development is also seen in other factors and aspects of growing and playing such that "plays well with other children" evolves into the child becoming a great team member.

The capacity to successfully navigate each competition level is not correlated specifically to chronological age. Developmental age is much more important. A participant's capacity is comprised of a unique mix of readiness, maturity, physical development, and the ability to learn. Competing at each particular level will demand its own set of required characteristics and elements. Everyone cannot reach every level. Not all of us end up skiing in the Olympics or swimming the English Channel.

We have deliberately focused on the characteristics of competition to describe each level rather than categorize it based on the age of the participants. This permits the participant to be the focus. Participants need to be able to compete healthily at each level. Each level contains its own unique set of constraints and complexities that challenge and develop the person.

Level 1: Experiential

    status of the individual: the person
    people involved: family, neighborhood, friends
    when: before any sports activity
    competition status: none
    parental role: role model and playmate

At this stage, we must add another *P*, for primacy. Everything for the person at this time is being done for the first time. If we consider games of low organization to be the first sports activities, then we may look at activities before them that involve interaction between parent and child as part of the child's growth and learning. Peekaboo would be one of these activities. There is an intrinsic joy of play between infant and parent.

In other words, youngsters have many primary experiences that are not sports. Some of these may be recalled at an older age. However, we

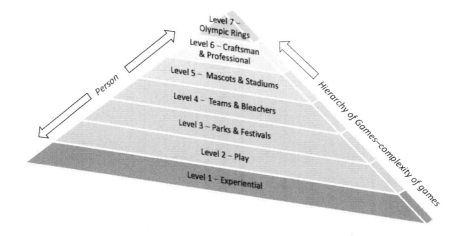

Taxonomy of competition. *Courtesy of Peter J. McGahey and Peter S. Pierro*

can make the case that the feelings acquired at this stage can affect our choices about what we like and what we don't like at later stages in our lives. They may even affect our behavior and our actions relative to playing and watching games. Here is a scenario.

Joey is four years old and the son of an Italian American family living in a suburb of Chicago. Today his mother, Grace, his father, John, and his baby sister, Rita, visited his grandparents in the city. After dinner they all went down the street to John's cousin David's house.

David and his wife Debbie have a nice backyard, and he has cut a section of the long grass to form a boccie court. Some of their friends came over with their children, and the games began. Joey and the other kids watched the games at first as the adults took turns playing. Joey heard a lot of laughter, he saw a lot of movement, he felt a lot of happiness. He was aware that his mother and father were having a good time. In fact, everyone was having a good time.

Now it was the kids' turn. Joey and his cousin Benny and friends Patty and Danny were ready to play the game. The other kids had played before and David helped Joey as he was learning how to play. He learned fast and enjoyed it. Joey's brain recorded and stored all this information and these feelings. He may not be able to recall this episode in later years, but the feelings and awareness had been established and they would influence his interest in sports for the rest of his life.

Level 2: Playing

    status of the individual: the person, participating and playing
    structure of games and sports activities: games of low organization
    people involved: family, friends, teachers
    relationship with others: playing alongside and with others
    competition status: minor, no winners or losers
    parental role: awareness of activity is incidental and encouraging

Children compete when playing games such as hopscotch, jump rope, tag, musical chairs, sharks and minnows, 500, and many others. As in musical chairs, there is a winner or winners and a loser or losers. The game deals only with the participants who are involved in the game.

Winning and losing aren't a big issue. Usually there's laughter and then "Let's do it again!" No one gets laughed at or ridiculed. It was fun; now let's move on and have more fun. No individuals are designated losers or winners. There is little to no sense of a team. Everyone is part of the activity and engaged in the play. Rules constantly evolve and are established by the participants to make the game last longer or be fairer or more fun.

This level is a garden of learning and development. Participants are developing physically. They are learning to jump, run, fall, throw, dodge, dart, and so on. Solutions and strategies to the game are being developed. Social emotional skills are fostered. They are learning how to get along with others and how to overcome setbacks. They are learning the importance of playing fair.

Trophies or rewards are not required or recommended. The reward is skinned knees, a few bruises, and smiling faces. Being able to joyfully play a fun game or activity with and alongside your buddy or best friend is the best reward in the world.

Level 3: Parks and Festivals

    status of the individual: the person, participant to player
    structure of games and sports activities: more-organized structures
        and games
    entity involved: team or other organizing group
    relationship with teammates and opponents: playing with teammates
        and opponents

people involved: teachers, coaches, and parents

competition status: more competition present, some winning and losing

external recognition: appreciation and celebration

parental role: supporter, supervisor, and fan

application of appropriate skills and strategies: exploration, experiential, and creativity

Level 3 presents a crossroads of sorts. Organization and structure for the participants increases. This increased organization and structure occur both in schools and in youth sport organizations. Teams can be formed, and structures to compete are provided.

Level 3 provides an exciting opportunity for participants. Increased structure results in more complex game environments for the participants to explore. More organized games often mean opposition, or opponents, but this is not in the classic sense of a true adversary; it is more of a partner to play with and alongside.

Adults involved in youth sport organizations often promote a false sense of urgency to rush through level 3. This urgency is caused by viewing the youth sports experience through the adult lens of sport competition. Basically, adults strive to create adult versions of sport and competition—knockout tournaments—with adult game structures and rules. The game and operation become the primary focus as opposed to the participants, the children.

Level 3 demands a child-centered learning environment. These children are always the primary focus of our youth sports environments. What are their needs and wants? What's best for them? Establishing a child-centered learning environment is critical if we want the child to both enjoy the game and prepare for long-term participation. Keeping the child as the primary focus allows exciting competitive environments to be created at level 3.

Organization and game structures are modified to fit the players. Small-sided games are organized. Reducing the number of players participating simplifies the learning environment. This creates more repetition and interaction within the game. Rules are modified and adjusted to fit the players and to improve their opportunity to play and explore. Level 3 may be organized primarily in local parks or neighborhoods to maximize participation.

Competition will be introduced gradually. This will allow the child to experience games without any repercussions from the outcome. The participants are playing with each other and not for something or for any organization. The participants are striving to win without having to win. Level 3 properly implemented allows for winners and losers without labeling individuals as winners or losers.

Teams can be formed. Games will be played. Learning the rules and the flow of games is important. No standings should be kept. Festivals should be played in lieu of knock-out tournaments. This allows the players to have fun experiences without all the structure and necessity of being with the same group of people all the time. Coaches and teachers provide limited instruction, permitting the participants to experience the rules and flow of the games. Facilitating a developmentally appropriate and safe environment for participants maximizes opportunities for exploration and expression of personality. It is through exploration and experience that participants move along the path toward becoming a player.

Remember, learning is not a winning-or-losing proposition. Everybody needs to win in their own unique way. *Everybody!*

Level 4: Teams and Bleachers

status of the individual: the person, the player

structure of games and sports activities: organized games and structures

entity involved: team or other organizing group

relationship with teammates and opponents: playing with and for your teammates and against your opponents

people involved: family, coaches, officials, and friends

competition status: competition is present, winning or losing gains significance

external recognition: trophies, medals, connection, and significance

parental role: supporter and spectator

application of appropriate skills and strategies: acquisition of skill and strategy accompanies need to apply

Complexity of competition begins at level 4. Games and youth sports move out of the park and into the bleachers. Teams that represent entities are formed: the Westside School Bearcats, the Jackson Jaguars. A name on the front of the jersey appears and begins to matter.

Organizational complexity begins to increase. Games and tournaments are scheduled at venues that may have scoreboards and lights. Participants may be announced publicly and recognized as members of both the team and the organizing entity. This recognition is significant. This permits us-against-them competition to begin. Our team of players is competing against your team of players. The outcome of the game or contest gains importance.

There are winners and losers. A team is called a winner or a loser according to its performance. When the Bearcats lose, each Bearcat player is a loser. When the Bearcats win, each player is a winner. A player may lose some of his or her individual identity and be simply part of a team, however. For example, "Did the Jaguars win yesterday?" with no inquiry about individual players' performances.

More organized and adult setups or versions of games tend to bring tournaments and trophies, external recognition, and rewards for performance and winning. Teams and players receive trophies and medals. At level 4, these external rewards tend to be more important to adult social media than to the players' self-esteem.

Though the team tends to be the focus, individual growth and development matters at level 4. The acquisition and application of skills and strategies is important. The person is moving from being a participant to becoming a player.

For the player there is an increased focus on learning new skills and expanding existing skills. Players begin to have a responsibility to improve. Along with this acquisition of skill and strategy there is a new need for their appropriate application. Appropriate application of skills and strategies helps to create successful outcomes. Stated more simply, skill and strategy applied correctly help teams win.

A coach's role truly expands at level 4. Expanding skills and strategies call for guidance, feedback, and instruction. Coaches are now more involved in the process. No one wants or needs to be coached at musical chairs or sharks and minnows. Players competing at level 4 want and need to be coached.

Becoming a player means acquiring or having the required skill for a particular level of play and learning how to navigate the expanded competitive environment that level 4 offers. There is more external noise and pressure. These elements demand the individual's attention.

Key developmental factors take on additional importance. A player's readiness and developmental status matters. Emotionally, a player needs to be able to cope with the pressures that winning and losing bring. Social maturity and cognitive maturity are manifested in sportsmanship: learning how to compete fairly within the rules and being a good sport, that is, winning and losing graciously. A player needs to be physically mature and coordinated enough to healthily and safely compete. A player needs to be able to learn and adapt to the competitive demands.

The parents' role at level 4 continues to evolve. Parents are still spectators though sometimes they may try to help the coach make decisions relative to their own children. Families are an important support system to aid players on their journey. Support for the child is a priority. This will include navigating obstacles that the child will face. This guidance and support should not undermine or interfere with the coach.

As the competitive demands rise in level 4 for the players, it is likely that more player time will be committed to playing and practice requirements. This may involve travel and greater resource commitment from parents and families. Camp experiences are often required to improve the skills of the player and establish commitment to the team.

Teams at level 4 may be talent based. Some players may not be qualified to participate. In some cases, players or their parents may decide to modify or end their involvement in the sport because the stakes are too high or their interests are taking them in other directions.

Level 4 can go on for quite some time with many different sub-levels or iterations: youth sports, junior high, high school, elite youth sports, intramurals. Level 4 is likely to be the pinnacle for most kids.

A Good Source

Linda and Richard Eyre in their marvelous book *Teaching Children Joy* tell about a family that one of them grew up with. It seemed to be just an ordinary family with six children. Each of these children had their own personality, part of which was calmness, a sense of security. What was special was their love and acceptance of one other. They were always there, at every game, to support one another.

Our task as coaches is to encourage parents to support their young athletes. This is their real function and obligation: to unconditionally support their child in his or her goal whatever that may be. Remember, as winning and losing gain importance we need to avoid placing labels on people. Love your players for who they are and not for what they do. They are always a person regardless of the results of any game.

Level 5: Mascots and Stadiums

status of the individual: the person, the player, the performer

structure of games and sports activities: highly organized games and operations with media involvement

entity involved: team and community

relationship with teammates and opponents: playing with and for your teammates and against your opponents

people involved: coaches, teammates, administration and management, officials, family, friends, fans, and the community

competition status: competition is the focus, winning and losing are significant

external recognition: trophies, medals, awards, scholarships, endorsements, and status

parental role: supporter and spectator

application of appropriate skill and strategy: acquisition of skill and strategy accompanies demand to execute

Competition at level 5 gets supersized and glorified. Competitive complexity increases dramatically. Think of it as moving from cozy, neighborhood high school bleachers to stadiums with video boards, luxury boxes, and snazzy concession stands. There is pomp and circumstance in level 5 competition though many of the elements of level 4 remain.

The person continues, with both the player and the performer manifesting in level 5. The expectation is now for the person to both grow and develop as the player while the performer shines brightly under the glow of stadium lights, on television, and on an enlarged stage.

There is an increase in external rewards and recognition associated with level 5 competitions. Trophies, medals, sponsorship, fundraising, and scholarship dollars are at stake. The prizes connected to the performance of an individual or team demand polished execution and performances. The safety net for players and coaches becomes much smaller.

Playing time is earned. Playing time is competed for in practice. Teammates may in fact be competing with each other for the same position and the finite resource of playing time.

The importance of the name on the front of the jersey grows. Teams are often associated with the organization that they represent: the University of Hills Lions, Fencepost University Tigers, Island State University Longhorns, and so forth. Players can further lose their individual identity.

The team often represents a community. The performance of the team connects with the fabric and identity of an organization or community. Winning creates a winner and losing creates a loser. Communities can become defined by these results. An organization's personification of results increases the competitive pressure felt by athletes and coaches. Players themselves become associated with this winning and losing.

The coach's role continues to gain importance. Athletes need support and guidance. The player demands further acquisition and refinement of skills and strategies. Coaches and the athletes collaborate in this learning. The learning is focused on execution at the appropriate moment.

There is a real challenge and opportunity in performing under the watchful eyes of coaches, organizations, media, and fans. Helping players embrace this responsibility and celebrate its benefits is an important role of the coach at level 5. Coaches assist with the creation of the platform for the performer to safely emerge.

Tickets are sold. Family, friends, and fans show up at games to cheer and support their team. There is an expectation of high-level performance and entertainment. Parental relationships further evolve from the fan in the folding chair to the fan in the stands. Their support and love are provided to the person. They will have little influence over the player, the performer, or the coach.

Successful navigation of level 5 calls for the right balance of readiness and development. Few athletes reach this level of proficiency and performance. Athletes are still growing and maturing at this level, though more will be closer to the end than the beginning of their athletic career. Emotional maturity is paramount if they want to manage the external pressures.

Competing at this level is exhilarating. There is pressure and excitement. The need to improve is constant. Status is a by-product. Being part of a team that's connected to a community is amazing. Yet a simple fact remains: the person, the player, the performer should remain inspired by the joy of playing the game.

Level 6: Craftsman and Professional

status of the individual: the person, the performer, the player, the brand

structure of games and sports activities: professional sports activities and highly organized games and operations with media and entertainment focus

entity involved: team, organization, league, community, and personal brand

relationship with teammates and opponents: playing with and for (and against) your teammates and against your opponents

people involved: coaches, teammates, agents, management, media, officials, family, friends, fans, trolls, and the community

competition status: intense

external recognition: trophies, championships, awards, compensation, significance, a legacy, outside interests

application of appropriate skill and strategy: acquisition of skill and strategy required to advance and professionally develop accompanied by the need to execute

Athletes are now being paid to play the game. They are being compensated for their athletic talents, abilities, and performances. Competition is connected to organizations, leagues, and entertainment. The You is also an I. Players have become professional, and they have an allegiance to their team if one is involved. They also have a responsibility to themselves and their individual brand.

A professional has made an agreement with another entity: the organization. There is an understanding that the conditions in the agreement are negotiable. A place on the team and within the organization is connected to performance and fulfillment of agreed-upon terms—a contract. The name on the back of the shirt begins to matter as well. The game has become a vocation, a job. It's still a game but it is also a job.

The players and coaches are recognized figures. The players are connected to the jersey number that they wear, their organization, and their performances both individual and team. The community and public desire to share vicariously in the competitive team experience by wearing jerseys, waving flags, painting their faces and bodies in team colors. They call the team "my team" as they share their own analysis from their easy chair.

The players and coaches are craftsmen. They are judged and evaluated by their performances that happen on the biggest stage. The work on their craft and sport occurs out of sight of most people. The sight of the developmental struggle and process is the privilege of a chosen few: teammates, coaches, and trainers. The collective talents and abilities of the players, coaches, and the organization create a demanding developmental environment. There is collaborative and competitive effort to bring out the best in everyone.

Winning is crucial because losing is really losing. Winning and losing are both temporary and lasting. Certainly there is a next game to play, and those involved get to demonstrate their resolve and grit. However, level 6 results are connected to standings, playoffs, financial rewards, future contracts, championship seasons, and legacies. Winning and being labeled a winner both carry importance.

External pressures are in full swing at level 6. The person who has reached this level is both a top talent and a top competitor. His or her competitive journey has instilled critical pieces of the competitive puzzle along the way. Though this level will belong to only a very small percentage of the children who begin playing, a simple fact remains. The person, the player, and the performer, with all the associated complexities and pressures, is still playing a game.

Level 7: Olympic Rings

> status of the individual: the performer, the player, the person
> structure of games and sports activities: Olympic games and international competitions
> entity involved: country, team, sport federation

relationship with teammates and opponents: playing with and for
your teammates, playing for your country and against your opponents

people involved: country or nation, coaches, teammates, agents,
management, media, officials, family, friends, fans, trolls, and
community

competition status: permanent and enduring

external recognition: medals, trophies, a legacy

application of appropriate skill and strategy: acquisition of skill and
strategy essential and accompanied by the privilege of executing
under the pressure of a fleeting moment on the world stage.

In most sports, competing at the Olympic or international level is the
pinnacle of competition. Only the very best in their chosen sport are
selected to represent their nation.

Olympic and international-level competitions occur periodically to
celebrate the beauty and challenge of sport. They are the zenith of
athletic competition. They can be the fulfillment of a childhood dream
and personal goal. You are representing your entire country, your family, your team, and yourself by competing for a brief moment in time for
a lasting and enduring legacy.

Many of the factors and elements of competition remain: playing
with and for teammates; learning and applying new skills and strategies
to a more-complex environment; managing and balancing external pressures while striving to find joy in the moment. Irrespective of the level,
the joy of playing the game must be present.

This joy we take with us for the rest of our lives. Not everyone can
become a member of a Hall of Fame. But we can fall in love with our
games. Our joy can fulfill a lifetime of passion with our sport. This is a
passion that we will share and pass on to others. The joy of playing the
game is essential.

THE PLAYING FIELD

Games are the players' playing field. Players are the ones in the arena.
It is their extended playground and the space they will use to have
childhood experiences that they can recall happily the rest of their lives.

As coaches we are privileged to join our players on their sports journeys. We have a responsibility to look over the total environment, the playing space that the players are operating within, as they play their game. The creation of a positive and constructive playing environment permits our players to become the best version of themselves.

We have brought you some critical sports psychology concepts and ideas. These should help you have your players learn how to play the game better.

We will share a final starting line-up here: some very clear conditions that must prevail and guidelines you must follow if your players are to have a joyful and positive growth experience.

- The game is for the kids. We have said this over and over. Since this is true, let's live up to it.
- Kids are people too. Can we treat our kids as human beings who sometimes make mistakes but are doing their best? Bill Farnham, a counselor and coach, told us, "If we treated our best friends the way we treat our kids, we wouldn't have those best friends anymore and probably wouldn't have any friends at all."
- The coach's job is to make the game a good experience for the kids. The coach is a master link in the chain. He or she can be a model of good behavior and sportsmanship, can control the kids and the crowd, can deal effectively with improper behavior.
- Parents are partners with the coach in their kids' experiences. The game is a combining of the goals and aspirations of three elements: the kids, the coach, and the parents. They are *all* partners in the venture.
- Kids play better in a non-threatening, positive environment. That is a fact for all of us. We do better when someone is not continually on our back telling us how poor we are as a person and how bad our performance is. The psychological principles shared throughout this book are positive and human-oriented.
- Making mistakes is an important aspect of improving our performance. We all make mistakes as we learn new skills—that's part of the process. Learning from our mistakes is a lot better and easier when our mentor understands this and is showing us how to improve ourselves as a result of our less-than-perfect attempts.

- The coach must create his or her own successes rather than try to be successful through the kids.
- Every person is unique. There are no two people exactly alike so there are many times when we coaches must deal with each of our players in ways that match their unique qualities, strengths, or problems. One size does not fit all kids or their abilities, their goals, their ways of learning, their ways of looking at life. Isn't that wonderful?
- Kids are eager learners. They want to improve themselves and their skill at playing the game. Our job is to be constant encouragers of them in their growth in skills and understanding of the game.
- Kids are kids. They are not small adults. Sports is a venue that must be designed to enhance the childhood experience. In other words, don't coach the kids in such a way that you are allowing sports to deprive them of their childhood.
- Last but certainly not least, there are values for kids in sports besides winning. Can we reach those goals for our kids without having to win? Does our having to win prevent us from giving the kids great experiences in attaining these other values?

Coaching is a journey. It is a journey that takes many curves and twists. Learning and passion are our companions. Values and beliefs are our road signs and guideposts. Our underlying principles chart our course to creating a positive and enriching sports experience for *all* of our players. Success is a personal creation. It doesn't happen by accident.

A FINAL STORY

Let's recall Vince Lombardi. Coach Lombardi is one of America's most revered sports figures. Was he successful? We don't know. We don't know what his goals were. From our point of view, he was a great success as a football player and as a coach, but that is our perception. What were his dreams, his visions, his life goals? Only he and those who were close to him and loved him knew of his personal marks of success. We have the strong feeling from what we have read and heard of Lombardi that he felt that he was a successful player and coach, father and husband, religious person, and human being.

A good indirect way of considering his success achievement is to examine his ability to inspire his players. He was an excellent model. He inspired them to heights that they had not been aware of and made those heights accessible to them.

Inspiration is the highest level of motivation. How do we motivate our players? How do we inspire them? We motivate and we inspire only when we ourselves care enough to do whatever is necessary to reach our own dreams.

Youngsters are seekers. They want to know more about themselves and the world around them. We believe that each of us has great potential. We believe our players are in the midst of developing and realizing their potential and we can assist them in their endeavor.

Youngsters are dreamers and goal setters. They want to accomplish great things. Pull up alongside your players. Embrace the wonderful privilege and responsibility of coaching. Encourage your players to dream big. And Coach, you dream big right along with them. New limits and possibilities are waiting to be discovered by you and by your players.

We wish you the best of luck on your coaching journey!

EPILOGUE

We have given you a lot of messages in these chapters. There were commentaries based on uniqueness, creativity, joy, naturalness, psychology, and philosophy. As these messages were given, we were dealing with coaches, players, and parents of players. Those coaches were ourselves or coaches we have known or have learned about.

Be very clear that we were not talking about you. We haven't talked about you because we don't know you. We don't know what kind of leadership model you feel is best for you. We don't know what you believe about winning and losing. We don't know if you have found joy in your sports experiences. We don't know what you are seeking.

What we do know is that you are a unique person. You are a creative person. You are a natural person. You are a seeker. You also have psychological and philosophical beliefs that you live in accordance with.

What we hoped to do, among other things, was to have you go on a journey with us. We hope that during this journey you received some insight into how you deal with your mistakes and how you relate to your wins and your losses, to your good and bad experiences in sports, to all of your life experiences.

We hope that you have had a good experience with us and that you will have a great, productive life doing whatever brings you joy and fulfillment.

APPENDIX

Player Rights and Responsibilities

The right to be treated fairly.	The responsibility to treat others fairly.
The right to express my ideas and be listened to.	The responsibility to listen to others and consider the worth of their ideas.
The right to participate in class as a unique person and learner.	The responsibility to do my best.
The right to have good coaching.	The responsibility to cooperate with my coach.
The right to be safe.	The responsibility to follow safety rules and not to endanger other people.
The right to be treated with respect.	The responsibility to treat others with respect.
The right to have my personal belongings safe and unharmed.	The responsibility to leave other people's property alone unless I have permission.
The right to share in making decisions for the team.	The responsibility to act and think in a responsible manner and to allow others to have their opinions.

The right to learn and not be left out.	The responsibility to do my work to the best of my ability and to be a constant learner.
The right to be a member of the team.	The responsibility to be a trustworthy team member.
The right to have good playing equipment.	The responsibility to take care of the playing equipment.
The right not to be embarrassed or insulted.	The responsibility to not embarrass or insult others.

THE RIGHT TO EXPERIENCE THE JOY OF PLAYING.

_____

Signed by Player

THE RESPONSIBILITY TO MAKE THE BEST OF MY PLAYING
EXPERIENCE.

_____

Signed by Coach

ABOUT THE AUTHORS

Peter J. McGahey, EdD, is a teaching assistant professor of athletic coaching education at West Virginia University. He has degrees in educational leadership, physical education and sport coaching, human performance, and sport and communications. McGahey was a NCAA Division I and II women's head and assistant soccer coach for more than twenty years. He is a national instructor and scout for the United States Soccer Federation and has coached athletes all along the developmental pathway from grassroots to college, youth to high school, and TOP-Soccer to the Olympic development program. He has been on the faculty of Minnesota State University, Mankato; Central Michigan University; Saint Leo University; and the University of Tennessee, Martin; and he was awarded a varsity letter for each of his four years playing men's soccer at the University of Denver. McGahey has led and developed coaching education and player development programming at the local club, state, and national levels.

Peter S. Pierro, EdD, is a retired professor at the University of Oklahoma. He has degrees in history, psychology, and education from Northern Illinois University. He has also been on the faculty at Elmhurst College, Southeastern Oklahoma University, and Langston University. He is the author of several books on teaching and learning. Among other sports experiences, he played with the Will-Walt team in the Northern Illinois Fastball League, the Utica Yanks semiprofessional baseball team, and U.S. Navy and Illinois Valley Community College basketball teams. During World War II, he was selected to play on the all-star team on the U.S. Navy Tinian Island basketball team. He was also an individual bowling champion in his senior year at Northern Illinois University. He has taught at the elementary, junior high school, high school, and university level and has coached basketball, baseball, and softball at the child, youth, high school, and adult levels. He received a Distinguished Professor of the Year Award at Elmhurst College in Illinois and is a member of the Illinois Valley Community College Hall of Fame. Playing golf is his major sports addiction at this time.

Related Book by Peter J. McGahey and Peter S. Pierro

The Soccer Coach's Guide to Working with Players and Parents

Related Books by Peter S. Pierro

Free to Learn—Free to Teach
The Coach's Toolbox: Using Sports Psychology with Your Kids
Growing and Learning: Discovering Your Child's Unique Learning Style